AWAY WITH WORDS

Young Writers' 16th Annual Poetry Competition

It is feeling and force of imagination that make us eloquent.

How can I not dream while writing? The blank page gives a right to dream.

West Midlands

Edited by Michelle Afford

 Young**Writers**

First published in Great Britain in 2007 by:
Young Writers
Remus House
Coltsfoot Drive
Peterborough
PE2 9JX
Telephone: 01733 890066
Website: www.youngwriters.co.uk

SB ISBN 978-1 84602 814 4

Foreword

This year, the Young Writers' *Away With Words* competition proudly presents a showcase of the best poetic talent selected from thousands of up-and-coming writers nationwide.

Young Writers was established in 1991 to promote the reading and writing of poetry within schools and to the young of today. Our books nurture and inspire confidence in the ability of young writers and provide a snapshot of poems written in schools and at home by budding poets of the future.

The thought, effort, imagination and hard work put into each poem impressed us all and the task of selecting poems was a difficult but nevertheless enjoyable experience.

We hope you are as pleased as we are with the final selection and that you and your family continue to be entertained with *Away With Words West Midlands* for many years to come.

Contents

Castle High School

Codsall Middle School

Edgecliff High School

George Salter High School

Sherilyn Gwen Smith (11)	75
Sarah Cumberlidge (15)	76
John Richards (15)	77
Christopher Griffin (15)	78
Jak Garrity (15)	79
Daniel McDonald (15)	80
Babley Zaman (11)	80
Sonia Nath (15)	81

Hagley RC High School

Catherine Coakley (14)	81
Katie Conlon (14)	82
Jennifer Barry (13)	82
Greg Humphries (13)	83
Whitney Rowles	83
Robyn Brooks	84
Daniel Cullen (13)	84
Danny Cameron (14)	85

Henley-in-Arden High School

George Meadows (13)	85
Katie Sheridan (13)	86
Caroline Curry (13)	87
Becky Gee (13)	88
Shaun Parsons (13)	89
Alex Stimpson (13)	90
Hannah Roberts (13)	91
Ryan Harvey (13)	92
George Wilson (13)	92
Emily Hancock (11)	93
Elizabeth Hansen (14)	94
Eleanor Wilson (13)	95
James Elliott (13)	96
Lauren Haslam (13)	97
Kayleigh Bradley (14)	98
Katie Brinkworth (13)	99
Daisy Smith (13)	100
Chloe Harrison (13)	101
Amey Walker (13)	101
Emily Allen (13)	102
Zoë Gardner (13)	103

The Poems

The Day That Has Changed The World Forever

The sky filled with smoke,
My eyes with tears,
We all stood still,
With uncertainty.

Silence in the beginning,
Hearing only my own heart,
My own breath,
Both getting faster.

Around me a woman holding her baby,
Closing her eyes in disbelief,
Next to her, an elderly couple,
Huddled together in fear.

Weeping. Screaming, Outcries.
Noise is now occurring,
All around me. And thoughts race through me,
Ones I cannot even begin to explain.

I look around me and suddenly,
Everything moves in slow motion,
The world seems surreal and
Fear sweeps through me.

I cry. Not in fear or shock,
But for the people in that building,
For the lives being lost
And for the people who have no hope left.

Nobody will ever forget this memorable day,
When families were lost. Mothers will say
To their children and grandchildren,
'Our husbands went to Heaven,
On that hateful day,
9/11.'

The sky still fills with smoke,
My eyes still with tears,
We all stand together,
Wounded.

Gabriella Hull (16)

Sunflower

As the sunflower sways side to side,
Other flowers watch its beauty and divine,
It shines in the dark night's sky,
As the moon glistens on its side.

Roses and bluebells try to look the same,
But something isn't right, they haven't got the name,
In the morning, the sun rises up high,
Spreads happiness to all of the flies.

As people watch the flowers,
They make beautiful smiles.

But now as the watery ice has come,
Flowers will go beneath the water's rush.

Shivani Pushkarna (13)
Alumwell Business & Enterprise College

My View Of The World

The world is small and glad,
No one here is sad,
Loads of people, loads of places
And loads of happy faces.

But things aren't always as good as they can be!
The waste, the pollution makes most people feel unhappy,
So help the environment, it'll be good for you and me,
Together we can protect the world and community.

This is my view of the world,
Telling people that things aren't always as
Bad as they can be!

Kiran Yusif (13)
Alumwell Business & Enterprise College

Summer's Day

As the sun shines,
Beneath the cloud its rays,
Bring smiles to people's faces,
In such lonely cases.

When you go for a walk all alone,
Remember you won't smile all alone,
Someone is really kind,
Up above sky like an angel of light,
Keep in mind,
It disappears at night.

As it shines in the sky,
People look up and feel the vibe,
Flower standing there all alone,
Give them company with a smile,
Just keep in mind,
Someone is really kind.

Neila Akhtar (13)
Alumwell Business & Enterprise College

Music

Music, music, everywhere,
Always in my head, here and there,
From the deepest depths of Hell,
Music is played very well
And all the way up above,
Music is played with lots of love.

Adam Townsend (13)
Alumwell Business & Enterprise College

Poems - My View Of The World

The sky is blue,
The grass is green
And a bluebird is seen.

I see a cloud,
It looks bright white,
Look up in that tree,
I can see a colourful kite.

Buzzy bees all flying around,
I see a honeycomb,
It falls to the ground.

I see insects flying in the air,
Oh look,
I see a bear.

Do you believe me?
Because it's true.

Emma Powell (12)
Alumwell Business & Enterprise College

Four Seasons

Seasons, seasons, there are four,
At different times of year,
They appear at your door,
Winter is the coldest and
Summer is the hottest,
Spring and autumn are full of change,
So let's celebrate all four.

Mohammed Zaeem (13)
Alumwell Business & Enterprise College

If I Could Change The World

If I could change the world,
It would be perfect,
There would be pink flowers everywhere
And I wouldn't care,
We would all be nice.

If I could change the world,
There would be no fights
And we would have rights,
Girls and boys would play together.

But I can't change the world,
It will never be perfect
And we will never get on,
There will always be fights
And will we never get rights?

Emily Burton (13)
Alumwell Business & Enterprise College

Dancing

My favourite dance style is Asian,
We move around slowly,
But sometimes we go fast,
I like to dance to English music as well,
My sister joins in with me,
The beat of the music in our ears,
We wear bright clothes
And have lots of fun.

Shahin Mohamad (13)
Alumwell Business & Enterprise College

Killer Whale - Haikus

Big black killer whale
That lives in a blue ocean
Eats tiny fishes!

Most are black and white
Squirting water all day long
When it comes to dawn.

Shelana Brooks (13)
Alumwell Business & Enterprise College

Day In Colours

Today is red, it's going to be dangerous,
I better go to the kirkyard,
As I get there, the day goes from blood-red to lemon-yellow,
I'm safe,
At last,
It's quiet,
Too quiet,
The blood is curdling,
It's coming after me,
I hear voices,
They want the kirkyard,
They want to take it from me,
They want the graves,
They want the tree,
This is my place, not theirs,
'Get lost,' I say, 'get lost!'
My day changes,
The lemon disappears,
The blood is back,
I go home,
He shouts, he wants the booze,
He swings,
He hits,
I'm out cold!

Janay Michael (12)
Bristnall Hall Technology College

Graveyard

I walk through the gates,
The terrifying screech of the gates makes me nervous,
It's like a car slamming the brakes on,
The headstones are all staring at me,
I can't take it,
I run to the empty part of the garden,
I wonder why nothing is here except a rowan tree,
Its silver bark,
Shimmers in the dark,
I have a hiding place,
Where nobody can see my face,
I pull back the rocks,
To get to my stash,
This graveyard is full of mist,
But it doesn't bother me,
I've been here many times,
Now it's time to leave
And go home and watch TV with my dad.

Andrew Hill (12)
Bristnall Hall Technology College

The Graveyard

Dusty ash floats below my feet,
Willow trees with reaching arms,
That snatch you into the endless night.

The dusk evening glow emphasises the perimeter
Of each gravestone in its solitude,
The eternal loneliness of this place is all around,
As the faint whispering of the eerie
Air fills my ears . . . in the distance, but now so loud . . .

Emma Wilkins (13)
Bristnall Hall Technology College

Whispers In The Graveyard!

I am the rowan tree,
I sit in the corner of my kirkyard,
I protect my territory
And listen to the whispers in the graveyard.

I ward off evil that dooms the night,
I am as delicate as a flowing kite,
I do not know how many days until the end,
But I have been here for years, I can't pretend.

I have seen the way that many people come and go,
But the wind, it blows me to and fro,
My roots, they spread under the ground,
But to your ears, you won't hear a sound.

My branches, they spread out wide,
So from the sun, you can hide,
In the summer, my leaves are green,
Looking at me then, I look so clean.

In the summer on the ground,
There are always flowers to be found,
Now it is time for them to go,
This time I'll take for me to grow.

Sometimes the rain is like a shower,
But I'll be here, I stay around,
I'm special you see, I have my power,
But if you look, it can't be found.

The gates are closed, I am locked away,
For no eyes to see, I'm kept at bay,
One person comes, he's only a boy,
I wish his pain was only joy, when he hugs me I feel his pain,
One day soon, I hope to see him soon.

Gemma Cox (12)
Bristnall Hall Technology College

The Rowan Tree

I'm old, I'm lonely, and nobody comes to me,
Only the spirits get to see me angry,
Oh but there was this boy,
He had a part of evil,
He tried to hug me,
I blew him away quickly,
Whoosh, whoosh, whoosh,
My vines are curled up,
Like a Curly Wurly chocolate bar,
My leaves are horrid,
Grey and green,
No birds come to me,
No nests either,
There are no berries on my branches,
My bark is crinkled, like a scrunched-up paper ball,
My roots are long,
Dug into the ground,
My life is ending soon . . .
I'm old, I'm lonely, and nobody comes to me.

Cherelle Poole (12)
Bristnall Hall Technology College

Dyslexia

I sit in the classroom,
Waiting for my work,
But when the work comes, I can't read it,
The words are slithering off the page,
The numbers are crawling off the sheet,
The teacher is coming,
I try to ignore him,
But he always gets in my head,
I can't block him out,
Because his voice is too strong,
So I retreat to my refuge, the kirkyard.

Ryan Wood (12)
Bristnall Hall Technology College

The Graveyard

I walk past the graveyard,
All dark and gloomy,
I feel and hear the wind as it whistles past my face,
I feel scared, terrified even,
I see a shadow, it's not mine,
I look behind me,
All is see is the graveyard,
I decide to go and have a look,
All I see is tombstones,
I hear a voice
And it's not mine,
It's coming closer,
I feel scared,
I'm surrounded by gravestones,
I don't know what to do,
I fall over a rock and hit my head,
Then I see red stuff dripping from my forehead,
Suddenly, I feel a hand on my shoulder,
I turn back, I see a skeleton,
I run off home,
I try to forget all about it,
I can't, it still frightens me,
I will never forget it.

Arundeep Shoker (12)
Bristnall Hall Technology College

My Brother

Brothers, brothers are all the same,
Brothers, brothers, they drive you insane,
My brother screams and starts to shout
And starts crying at the sight of sprouts,
My brother, he likes wrestling,
He always has the need to start pestering,
Brothers, brothers, they're all the same,
Brothers, brothers, they drive you insane.

Ifra Ahmed (13)
Bristnall Hall Technology College

The Rowan Tree

I am a rowan tree,
I stroll through the kirkyard warding off evil,
The wind blows the leaves off me,
I stand in the kirkyard alone,
There is no one else around me
Apart from the cold headstones,
There's no one else but me,
My kirkyard is cold and I am alone,
I stand in the cold and listen to the whispers,
The sun never shines in this part of the kirkyard,
It is always dark and cold,
I wish I was in a park with the sun gleaming
And the children running towards me,
What else is there for me in this kirkyard?
This kirkyard is so ancient,
There is nothing else for me as they are chopping me down,
The young boy Sol will be so upset, he was my only friend.

April Brandon (12)
Bristnall Hall Technology College

A Night Spent On The Streets

A night on the streets is frightening,
You can't get a decent night's sleep,
Whenever I close my eyes I hear people shouting,
How would you feel sleeping in the cold?
Would you be scared someone might leave you for dead?
I try to keep awake,
Listening to the clock tick,
As time passes,
I hear drunken people,
Cars driving by,
I can hear my belly rumbling,
As I close my eyes,
That's another rough night's sleep.

Nitin Kaushal (14)
Bristnall Hall Technology College

The Rowan Tree

Here I am, swaggering in the wind,
I'm lonely, I'm lonely,
My ugly, grey green leaves,
I'm ugly, I'm ugly,
Curly, skinny vines get tangled
And stuck, and stuck,
The evil spirits bellowing to me,
They're evil, they're evil,
They keep coming and calling,
I don't listen, I don't listen,
My roots frozen still into the dark, dead soil,
I'm old, I'm old,
Everything's still, deserted,
I shiver, I shiver,
Just a small leaf scatters along my feet,
I'm cold, I'm cold.

Here I am, swaggering in the wind,
I'm lonely . . .
I'm lonely . . .

Chloe Ramsbottom (12)
Bristnall Hall Technology College

Warrior Watkins

Warrior Watkins, my teacher,
To me he's extra mean,
That's only on the days that I am seen,
I bunk off school quite often,
The work is really hard,
I go and sit alone in the local kirkyard,
The graves in here are ancient,
I sit alone by the dreary rowan tree,
There's nobody up here . . . no one but me!

Sophie Gordon (13)
Bristnall Hall Technology College

The Shame!

I dreaded walking through the door,
As I walked I looked at the floor,
I glanced up to see if he had any more
And yes, two bottles, and more I'm sure.

He glared at me, anger in his eyes,
His rage, to me, was no surprise,
So I walked backwards towards the stairs,
As he rose from his chair.

He shouted, his voice alerted danger,
The violence he gave was no stranger
And as his arm pulled back, fist clenched,
I ducked the pain that he quenched,
I wouldn't satisfy that need,
I wouldn't let him make me bleed.

Again! No! No more pain!
So I ran, from my dad . . .
The shame.

Casey Cole (12)
Bristnall Hall Technology College

Dyslexic

My days are getting worse,
My Bs and Ds, 9s and 6s,
Are getting very blurred.

People call me stupid,
The time is dragging by,
No matter how hard I try,
People still think I'm stupid.

Dyslexic is what they call me,
It's one of the names I've got,
No one's there to help me,
So I'm stuck here with this lot.

Gemma Holly Thomas (12)
Bristnall Hall Technology College

Drunken Colours

My days are great when rosy pink,
Calm and sweet,
No need to think,
About what it's like to live with you.

Happiness spells my days blue,
The days I am away from you.

Nervous paints the colour green,
As it eats away at me like a maggot,
At a sandwich, as I wonder where you've been.

Crazy confusion paints it yellow,
It's fun whilst you're still mellow,
But it's not long before I see your drunken shadow.

My dull days equal brown,
The most common day,
When I'm feeling down.

Shocking paints the day white,
Seeing the state you're in gives me such a fright.

Crashing anger turns it red,
So I snuggle down in my bed.

When I'm scared, it's black,
As I sit awaiting your drunken smack.

My life is a rainbow,
Colours flying in and out,
Whilst living with a drunken lout.

Natalie May Turton (12)
Bristnall Hall Technology College

Poem

You went away,
But only for a day,
You came back, I walked away,
Oh I wish I could tell you why.

Sometimes you're on my mind,
Only when I close the blind,
So I know I don't have to find,
Something else for my mind.

I took a love test
And it looked like we matched,
I thought that the memories we had,
Were better washed away.

But now I hope,
That every lesson learnt,
You might just see that we belong
And that nothing stops me loving you.

And with us far away,
Forever love will stay,
Keep this loving feeling inside,
Forever and always.

Whenever dark turns to night
And all the dreams sing their song
And in the daylight forever,
To you I belong.

Chelsea Maynard (15)
Bristnall Hall Technology College

Whispers In The Graveyard

I come from school all black and blue,
I've been confused, more like rouge,
The day continues when I get home.

I get home with nothing to eat,
Not even something sweet,
I feel as thin as a bone.

So I run to my sanctuary,
Known as the kirkyard,
Where the whispers lie in the graveyard.

I clamber over the wall,
To find something extremely tall,
Amongst the undressed open yard.

The rowan tree standing so tall and brave,
The many precious lives he has saved,
But no one is yet to reciprocate him.

I approach the rowan tree full of emotion,
As his mercy, with devotion,
I plunge back with a slashed limb.

I understand why he is down and blue,
But his infective aura is dawning on me too,
I know what I have to do and I have to do it soon . . .

Nikita Dosanjh (12)
Bristnall Hall Technology College

Nobody Loves Me

My mommy doesn't love me,
Why else would she make me suffer?
She tells me I've been naughty
And I have to learn my lesson.

My daddy doesn't love me,
Why else would he make me scream?
Hit me hard with a broken bottle
And say I was a mistake.

My mommy doesn't love me,
Why else would she make me cry?
Scratch me deep with her long nails
And call me a sinner.

My daddy doesn't love me,
Why else would he kill me?
Kick me until I scream no more
And cannot breathe another breath.

My parents didn't love me,
For me it's too late now,
Don't let kids like me suffer,
So give money and give us kids hope.

Gurbinder Manku (14)
Bristnall Hall Technology College

Colours

I walk into school, is it going to be a blue day
Or an angry red?
I walk into Warrior Watkins' lesson,
He comes straight over,
His face peers down at me,
The little red broken vein's about to burst,
I look up,
His eyes look fierce, like when a tiger is about to pounce,
He has a firm grip on his ruler,
Thump, thump,
He can't hit me, can he?
Watkins begins to shout.
The words hit me like bolts of lightning!
He then shouts, *'Out!'*
I stroll out of the playground, towards the kirkyard,
I climb over the graveyard wall,
I feel safe,
At last,
I go to my place and read my comic,
I close my eyes,
Today has gone from an angry red to a cool, calm blue,
Will tomorrow be the same?
Who knows?

Charlotte Malley (12)
Bristnall Hall Technology College

Age Poem

When I was one, I had just begun,
When I was two, I was nearly new,
When I was three, I was hardly me,
When I was four, I was not much more,
When I was five, I was hardly alive,
But now I am six, I'm as clever as clever,
So I think I'll be six for ever and ever.

Michelle Reed (12)
Bristnall Hall Technology College

What Am I?

I worry each morning as the sun breaks through,
With my life, what else am I supposed to do?
I get out of bed and prepare for school,
But at this place I'm taken for a fool!
As I reach the school gates and see my mates,
I get a cold feeling down my spine,
When I walk in the classroom it looks like a hole of doom
And so the taunts begin,
I can't read or write and I feel so dumb,
I can't even say a simple sum!
When I'm older, I'll have to get a job,
This will be a mission, what should I say?
What should I do?
Maybe one day education will go *Boo, I'm here for you,*
But for now, I still have that certain condition
And it won't let me be clever,
It begins with d.
Surely you can see what the condition is . . . ?
What is it?
What am I?

Luke Hibbs (12)
Bristnall Hall Technology College

Help Us!

Locked away in a dark, gloomy room,
Left scared and alone in a certain doom,
No water to drink and no food to eat,
All alone and can hardly stand on my feet.

My owners have gone and left me alone,
My friend Chesney is turning to bone,
All alone and nothing to do,
My owner has left me to sleep in my poo.

Josh Hawkins (14)
Bristnall Hall Technology College

Golden Lady

As the cool autumn breeze blows over the cobbled path,
The moon's glorious rays walk the grass,
Touching every piece of marble and stone,
The long silenced pictures lay there cold and emotionless,
Except for one,
The moons tops, highlighting the large angel monument,
Bringing it back to its former glory,
The large golden angel stands with her ivory doves circling her body,
The midges hover overhead, alive and happy,
The crisp golden leaves from the rowan tree fall to the
Ground all around her,
As she stands in her splendour, she looks out at the graveyard,
The sky-blue hummingbirds in their wooden nest,
The prickly hedgehog sleeping in the leaves,
But as the morning comes, the silence will end!

Felicity Hall (13)
Bristnall Hall Technology College

Graveyard

White mist slowly slides across the dark ground
Like a blanket of silk,
Trees claw like tigers, air's stench is like bad milk,
Tombstones rise like crooked teeth,
My senses drift across this deathly heath,
I'm scared, I'm sick, I want to vomit,
Fear smashes my soul like a rogue comet,
Will I survive the night to be back at home
Or will I be destroyed like the walls of Rome?
Please God, please save my soul,
I don't want to be in a six-foot hole,
What was that sound? Was it a spectre?
I should run a mile . . . no make that a hectare,
The cold hand of the Reaper is squeezing my heart,
I'm tasting death and it tastes tart.

Samuel Jukes (12)
Bristnall Hall Technology College

Sometimes I Wish I Wasn't Famous

Everyone thinks being famous is cool,
Sometimes it is, others it's a drool,
From adoring fans wanting your autograph,
To the impatient press wanting your photograph,
Don't get me wrong, I love all the attention,
But sometimes it feels like I'm in detention,
I can't escape from this feeling,
I think my life needs some healing,
Everywhere I go someone shouts my name,
Hundreds of people rush over all wanting the same,
Having all this money is great,
But sometimes I just feel I need a mate,
My life is OK,
But I have one thing left to say . . .
Sometimes I wish I wasn't famous!

Katy Allen (13)
Bristnall Hall Technology College

In The Graveyard

In the graveyard there is nothing at all,
Except a few headstones standing tall
And the gentle breeze's calming hush,
I trudge through the grass all green and lush,
The branches of trees reach out to get me,
But at the back of the graveyard,
There is just a single rowan tree,
Surrounding the tree the land is all bare,
I gaze at the sky and the moonlight's stare
And the stars scattered across the night
And I think to myself *what a beautiful sight*,
I look down to earth and the mist swirls between graves
And across the kirkyard the shadows wave,
In the graveyard there is nothing at all,
Except a few headstones standing tall.

Stephen Hill (12)
Bristnall Hall Technology College

The Graveyard

Pushing open the stone-cold gate,
I suddenly feel very queer,
Nothing but stones litter the floor,
It's the only quiet place around here.

Looking up to the moonlit sky,
I get a shiver up and down my back,
Shuffling my feet over to the den,
I sit down and open my sack.

What shall I have today then?
Apple, biscuits or some cheese?
In the distance I hear the rowan tree,
That's waving and rustling its leaves.

What is that that I hear?
People are coming this way,
They're on about digging up graves,
They're thinking of starting today.

Suddenly I feel all alone inside me,
Salt tears trickle down my face,
I think some sort of danger is coming,
I don't know what I'll do if I lose this place.

Charlotte Jones (12)
Bristnall Hall Technology College

A Night In The Cold

The time has come again,
Time to lie in the freezing cold,
Listening to the slightest noise,
Counting the hours as they pass by.

Tossing and turning all night long,
Hoping to get comfy and warm,
But it doesn't work,
Not even a bit.

Counting the bruises,
One by one,
Dying for food
And praying for tomorrow.

Wondering what's happening
And lying there in despair,
That's when depression and loneliness kicks in,
Praying for the company.

Preparing for the begging tomorrow,
Lying on the hard floor,
Freezing cold and really hungry,
Hoping that no one attacks me.

Jamie Williams (13)
Bristnall Hall Technology College

A Poem About A Night Spent On The Streets

In the doorway, you're alone,
You lay on the floor of stone,
As you toss and turn, you mutter and moan,
Because you're thinking of your home,
Your things get stolen,
You want to go back to your home,
Mum and Dad, I think this is mean,
I'll always be with you in my dreams,
You sit there on your own, aching,
In the freezing cold, shaking,
You're scared of everyone, you're on your own,
Things like this make you miss home,
Shelter is what you need to find,
But there are also other things on your mind,
Determination of the strong,
Will help you find the thing you searched for for so long,
Your clothes are ripped, you have nothing to wear,
You think this is a nightmare,
So you're all alone
And you hope one day you'll find a place to call home.

Jason Cotton (13)
Bristnall Hall Technology College

Homeless

I am homeless in a way,
On the streets every day,
People walk by,
Stop and stare,
Then walk on like I'm not there.

You don't know what will happen at night,
You just lay there filled with fright,
Hoping morning will come quick,
So you are sure that you're safe and fit.

Then you start to miss home,
Because at least there you were safe and warm.

Saphira McIntosh (13)
Bristnall Hall Technology College

Wonder

Have you ever wondered what it's like to fall
And keep on falling and never stop?
Have you ever wondered what it's like to die but
You never want to find out?

You just keep on wondering and wondering,
But what happens when you wonder too much
And you find yourself in a situation?

Maybe you're on a train track in a tunnel,
Standing on the metal rails,
Then you hear the noise, see the lights
And you try and save yourself as if your arm
Is going to stop 20 tonnes of metal and wheels.

You feel the wind rush across your face,
You crouch down and feel the wheels rush over you
And then you think,
So this is what it's like . . .
Death.

You think, *why isn't it painful?*
But then you find you can stand
And you look across to the other track,
Where your whole family were stood
And you wish you'd never looked
And you wish you'd never wondered,
So you try not to think of it every minute,
Every hour and second of every day,
Every little crack of your life you just try not to think
And not to wonder . . .

Ella Beard (12)
Bristnall Hall Technology College

Hurt

I lie in fright, every night,
Because they've all gone out,
They finally come, him and my mum
And start to scream and shout.

I pull the covers over my head,
But he comes in and drags me out of my bed,
I'm on the floor,
He's closed the door
And nobody says anymore.

Morning's here
And I'm shaking with fear,
Wondering if he's going to hurt me,
He doesn't say a word,
But I'm still scared,
Because what he's doing is dirty.

Taberah Khan (13)
Bristnall Hall Technology College

A Day Spent Begging

'Change please Sir,'
He just walks on by,
But the thing is, I don't see why,
Everyone's the same,
They just think we're playing a game,
It's like I'm not there,
No one even stops to stare,
Rumbling tummy
And I don't have any money,
As the day comes to an end,
I count my money
And it's not funny,
To have to beg like me!

Charlotte Jones (13)
Bristnall Hall Technology College

Home Today, Homeless Tomorrow

I didn't choose to beg,
I had no choice,
People stare,
What a nightmare.

The nights are the worst,
You don't know what's going to happen,
Kids staring,
Adults glaring,
You shiver.

You try to smoke the pain away,
Day after day,
Every day hassles,
Depression and despair.

Your face all dirty,
Your nails all chipped,
People staring as if you're lying,
Can't they see no food means dying?

I asked some guy for some money,
He replied by saying, 'That's so funny,'
He carried on walking and laughing too,
I then shouted, 'I really hate you!'

I feel so lonely,
Nothing to do,
When no one can see you,
What's the point of trying?
No money,
No food,
You don't want to be rude.

I didn't choose to beg,
I had no choice,
Ah, here we go again.

Jackie Abbey **(13)**
Bristnall Hall Technology College

A Day Spent Begging

I didn't choose to become homeless and beg,
I didn't want to leave home but I had to,
It's hard to ask for money but you have to,
If you want to live and eat,
You have to get used to the idea of begging
And being homeless.

You have to go out early and swap places in the day,
So people don't recognise you,
You would hate it if you had to ask people for money
And they said, 'No chance,' or just ignored you.

You are happy if it is only a couple of pence,
If you don't earn any money in one place, move to another place,
You have to watch out other beggars don't see you or they
Will either steal your money or ask the person before you do.

As the day finishes and the sun goes down,
The streets become quieter and not many beggars are around,
There is not much point in staying around and waiting for people,
You find somewhere to go and sleep for the night.

Neil Bate (13)
Bristnall Hall Technology College

Standing In The Graveyard

Standing in the graveyard, amongst all the graves,
I can hear every whisper, from the people who lay here,
The little voices give me comfort from the dead,
Reassuring the messages, answering the questions in my head,
There is a soldier, next to him lies his friend,
A tiny little child and a man with no name,
I fear nothing as I wander with the past,
They are only our loved ones asleep under grass,
As I take comfort in the silence, I remember all I knew,
Then when you are asleep, hope that someone thinks of you.

Peter Jelf (12)
Bristnall Hall Technology College

To A Dog In Need, You're A Friend Indeed!

I lie in my basket, wagging my tail,
Hidden in the warm from the snow and the hail,
Thinking of my friend outside in the sleet,
I snuggle down deeper, making the most of the heat.
When I'm just getting comfy the door opens wide,
In comes my friend, I run to his side,
He lifts me up and strokes my back,
Then he wraps me in a blanket and into his rucksack,
He goes back out the door with me in his bag,
But as we get in the car he removes my tag,
He finally stops and we get out of the car,
I'm freezing out here but we don't walk far.
He takes me out of the bag and puts me onto the floor,
Then he ties me up, slamming the car door,
I bark after him, I wonder if I've been bad,
I thought that he loved me so now I feed sad,
I lie down on the ground, and then I see a bright light,
There's a man coming nearer, I quiver with fright.
But he picks me up and holds me tight,
He's keeping me warm on this cold night,
He takes me away to a warm cosy bed,
Where I lie in a basket and rest my head,
This place I am now is the RSPCA,
I've been here a week, I'm going up for adoption today!
So if you feel sorry about the story I've told,
Then donate £2 a month and stop other dogs being cold.

Holly Henderson (13)
Bristnall Hall Technology College

My Cousin Neil

Neil is my only treasure to me,
He really means a lot,
One day I said, what will I do without you in my life?
I can't believe you disappeared without saying goodbye,
Now I've got to live my life without you by my side,
But I have to try and be brave,
Because without you, life is not the same,
You're in my heart,
You're in my brain,
Looking up at you in the sky,
Watching the clouds go floating by,
Loving memories fill my head,
Thinking of you peacefully when lying in my bed,
You made me laugh,
You made me cry,
You made the tears come from my eye,
Suddenly . . .
                    You're gone!
Rest in peace!

Tammy Micklewright (15)
Bristnall Hall Technology College

Poem

I'm all alone, sad and cold,
Nothing to be said, nothing to be told,
I sit and wait here day by day,
Waiting for someone to come my way!

But there's no sign of anyone around,
Not much earned, only a few pounds,
I'm sad and cold and down in the dumps,
With cuts and bruises and a few lumps.

Day and night I sit and cry,
Waiting for a miracle but not worth a try,
No one cares if I'm dead or alive,
But somehow I know I'll survive!

Lauren Rees (13)
Bristnall Hall Technology College

I Need

I need a new home,
I need a comfy bed,
I'm almost dead.

Help me please,
Help me please,
Help me please, I need some help.

People treat me like dirt
And I don't like it,
But all I can do is just sit.

Help me please,
Help me please,
Help me please, I need some help.

I need food,
Most people think that I'm to lend,
All I want is just one friend.

Gianpaolo Di-Vito (13)
Bristnall Hall Technology College

Calls For Help!

As it lies on the dirty kitchen floor,
A violent drunk comes through the door,
He walks! The kitten tries to hide,
Its mother, because of him, has tragically died.

He grabs the plate and throws it at the wall,
The kitten whines, for help it calls,
His eyes glare, he beats and kicks,
Its wounded leg, the kitten licks.

As the blood trickles down its leg,
It becomes desperate and starts to beg,
But luckily help arrives and the kitten's free,
Now a healthy kitten, you will see.

Sandeep Gahir (13)
Bristnall Hall Technology College

A Night Spent On The Streets

I lay there one night,
Trying to sleep,
When I heard footsteps,
But were they for me?

Then the footsteps stopped,
There wasn't a sound,
So I went back to
Trying to sleep on the ground.

I wish I was at home,
In my bed,
Like a bug in a rug,
My mom would have said.

I've got nothing to lose
And nothing to my name,
If my mom could see me now,
I'd bow my head in shame.

April Tucker (13)
Bristnall Hall Technology College

Da Door

As the years go by my hinges rust,
My gaps become blocked as they fill with dust,
My handle gets dirty from dirt and germs,
My windows are washed with mud and worms.

My locks grow weak as they are activated every night,
As I hang still from my hinges, I overhear a fight,
My windows are smashed from people banging into me,
Then they are replaced exactly as they used to be.

The texture of my coat is eroded by the Blu-Tack,
Then I become heavier when I am used as a coat rack,
As I become lonely I stand on the floor,
Always knowing I will just be da door.

Bruce Saleeb-Mousa (13)
Bristnall Hall Technology College

If I Died Tomorrow

If I died tomorrow,
Would you really care?
Would you stop and stare?
Would you realise I wasn't there?

If I died tomorrow,
What would you do?
What would you say?
What would you feel?

If I died tomorrow,
Would you be happy?
Would you be sad?
If I died tomorrow, it would be so bad.

If I died tomorrow,
Would you really care?
Would you stop and stare?
Would you realise I wasn't there?

If I died tomorrow,
Where would I be?
Where would I go?
Heaven or Hell, I don't know.

If I died tomorrow,
I wouldn't be there,
I would never be able to stare,
If I died tomorrow, could you really bear it?

If I died tomorrow,
How would you remember me?
How would you say,
That you loved me?
If I died tomorrow . . .

William Lane (13)
Bristnall Hall Technology College

The Legend Of The Sea

For what do the waves come hurtling to the shore
And why does the blue water splash the cliffs for evermore?
What secrets lie hidden on the mysterious sea floor?

This was a very long, long time ago,
Was there land beyond the sea? People were desperate to know,
When the mysterious blue water tempted sailors to swim away
And only hope was left in hearts that they'd return some day.

Once a brave soldier said to his beloved bride,
'I saw a glimpse of bliss in the turning, twirling tide,
I give my word I'll find it, beyond the dazzling blue,
Please wait for me beloved, I shall return to you.'

The vicious sea did not bestow the happiness he wanted,
It took his soul. And since the waves the soul has haunted,
Thus, the forlorn bride remained, wandering among the piers,
Until the sea turned salty from her never-ending tears.

In rage the sea had risen to take her broken heart,
From which all love was drained and from the soul it was apart,
No more she suffered from love and grief,
The sea turned her into a cliff.

Since then only waves come hurtling to the shore,
Meaninglessly they splash the cliff, seeking for the
Bride for evermore,
And slowly, the blue water goes back to the mysterious sea floor.

Kseniya Samsonik (12)
Bristnall Hall Technology College

The Rejected Cat

I was happy, I was brave,
But now they have taken it all away,
I'm as lonely as can be,
Nobody but me.

I cry and cry,
I wish I could have died,
To stop all this pain,
That's hurting deep inside.

How sad can you get
To make the owner regret,
All of the suffering and pain?

I might be a cat,
As normal as can be,
Why doesn't anyone love me?
It is because I'm thin and bony?
All I want is a home!

Nicola Avery (13)
Bristnall Hall Technology College

Untitled

I wish I knew what I'd done wrong,
I've been chained up for so long,
They seemed so happy when I was a pup,
But now when I bark, they just tell me to shut up,
They keep me chained to the garden shed
And only let me in to be fed,
I wish I knew what I'd done wrong,
I've been mistreated all life long,
My owner's have forgotten me
And all about my swollen knee,
All I need is to be loved,
But instead, in the shed I am shoved,
I wish I knew what I'd done wrong,
I really wish I knew what I'd done wrong.

Sam Bennett (13)
Bristnall Hall Technology College

That Cool, Cold Day

It was a cool, cold day,
When my master left me astray,
A blistering breeze blew over the moors,
It rattled the car doors,
Far away from the big city,
That's where my master dumped me.

I battled against the harsh gale,
I tried my hardest but to no avail,
And there I lay, I a little tabby,
On my own since I was a baby.

I was helpless, I was crying,
There on my back, I was lying,
Then came a girl, kind and jolly,
I was suspicious yet not wholly.

And that's how I met my new owner,
If only there were more people like Fiona,
We animals some people treat like dirt,
But we have feelings - we do get hurt.

Joseph Sturman (13)
Bristnall Hall Technology College

Imagination!

Along the corridor
And up the stairs,
A room awaits,
All dark and bare.

I approach the door,
Then stop and stare,
To find a woman standing there,
My heart pounds.

I open the door
And run straight in,
To my surprise I see something,
My mind goes blank.

The woman is there,
She stands and stares,
She walks straight through me,
Then I begin to see.

My mind made a creation,
The woman is my imagination.

Annisha Rukar (12)
Bristnall Hall Technology College

Our Class Today!

I wonder what the class will be like today,
It's totally brand new, as the head teacher did say,
Reece will be pulling silly faces at me,
Leanne will be laughing, so that everyone can see.

Carmel will be drawing, all alone in the back,
Mesha will scream and Dave will attack,
Kenny will pinch and pull Lesley's hair,
Gina will watch, she doesn't seem to care.

Rowan will be wrestling Alex to the ground,
The class today will make a terrible sound.

Amy will answer back when I try,
To explain basic algebra, then she'll ask why?
Rita will be polishing her nails again
And Peter will moan when I ask for a pen.

George will push Harry, and Harry will cry,
Then it will be chaos, oh why? Why? Why? Why?
Ben will bang Larry's head on the table
And Maddy will trip and fall over the cable.

Roy will come crying cos he has a cut
And Adam will faint cos he's allergic to nuts
And I will be thinking of how bad teacher could be,
But what it would be like without my class 6B.

Natasha Bigford (15)
Bristnall Hall Technology College

Sad, Afraid And Alone

We're going out today,
Just me and my good friend,
But she seems angry, nasty, uncaring,
When did her good mood end?

She used to be so nice to me,
Let me play outside till I was black as soot,
Now the only time she touches me,
Is when she kicks me with her left foot.

She's put me in a cardboard box,
With holes punched through the lid,
Why is she doing this, is it me
Or something that I did?

Now we're in the car,
Driving who knows where?
The box slides around, to and fro,
I call but she doesn't care.

She takes me out and sets me down,
On a cold, hard floor,
There's water underneath, it's seeping through
And chilling me to the core.

She's walked away, I heard her go,
She doesn't come back when I moan,
It seems as if she doesn't want me,
If she did, why did she leave me sad, afraid and alone?

Ruby Rowley (14)
Bristnall Hall Technology College

(Un)Lucky The Dog

They moved house yesterday,
The rain beating as I lay,
Upon the sofa of my old home,
Them waiting for the van man to phone.

I just had got off to sleep,
When I was pushed off into a heap,
'We'll come back later,' they said,
Closing the door, carrying the bed.

But they never did,
Not my friends or Uncle Sid,
I often wonder whether I was bad,
Or whether they really had.

But now I am in Heaven,
My friends are here too,
I am free and safe now
And I don't need you!

Louis Snookes (14)
Bristnall Hall Technology College

Help Dogs Trust

I'm small and defenceless,
Yet I'm treated so bad,
But here I am given the life I never had.

Dogs Trust care for me,
They give me love and care,
Inside Dogs Trust we are all treated fair.

I am free from the abuse and the names,
The shouts, the screams, the moans,
I'd know I was in trouble when I heard the groans.

Please help Dogs Trust,
Because they are helping me,
With your help and their help, I can be free.

Nina Purewal (13)
Bristnall Hall Technology College

Rejected

I am alone,
With just a sack,
I have no bone,
With no time to pack.

I was dumped,
By the side of a river,
I thought they cared,
But now I shiver.

I was betrayed
And now I scurry,
To find the unwanted,
Now's the time to worry.

I was treated badly,
Nobody cared,
I became devastated quickly,
I became unwanted.

I became neglected,
Kicked out,
I was always rejected,
Now all I smell is trout.

I am starving here,
With nothing to eat,
I wish they would hear,
But I'd rather be here than beat.

Now I am sinking,
Into darkness,
I am dying,
Into darkness I pass.

Ian Cree (14)
Bristnall Hall Technology College

Abandoned

When I was young I lived in a home,
It was cosy and warm
And I was never alone.

I had my own name,
I had my own bowl,
But now I know it will never be the same.

My life is now worthless and empty,
I have no friends
And everyone I see just stares at me.

My image is now just skin and bone,
I'm always cold
And I just want my home.

All I'm surviving on is water and grass,
I've got cuts and bruises,
Because I'm surrounded by glass.

That's because where I'm living,
Is a very dangerous place,
Even for a human being.

So please can you be generous and donate,
So Dogs Trust can save me,
Before it's too late.

Danielle Newman (14)
Bristnall Hall Technology College

Abused Kitten

Cold,
So cold,
Where am I? I can't see,
Help me please,
Find me quickly,
My back is cut,
My feet are torn,
I don't think you're coming, are you?
You never will,
If you can, though,
Stop this happening again . . .
Other little kittens . . .
Will appreciate it, like me,
I wish I could live . . . I want to see . . .
My own loving family . . .
So, please . . .
Help me!

Elizabeth Ormston (13)
Bristnall Hall Technology College

My Cat

My cat is as playful as a tiger,
She tries to camouflage herself in the grass,
As she watches her prey,
Then suddenly she . . .
Pounces at her prey!
My cat's colour and the look on her face,
Are the same as a koala bear,
She has an expression when she spots someone,
That says look but
Do not touch!

Richard Herman (11)
Castle High School

My Birthday

Hooray! It's my birthday,
The best time of year,
I wake up early and give out a cheer!
I go downstairs and what do I see?
Lots of presents waiting for me,
All of my family come round to see,
Me open my presents happily.

I go shopping the next day,
With my birthday money,
My friend comes too,
It is really funny,
We eat lots of chocolate up Merry Hill,
My mate has too much
And makes herself ill.

But in the end we had a great time
And now that's the end of my rhyme.

Billie Tennant (12)
Castle High School

You

Love never played a big part in my life,
But now I've met you, it's taken on a whole new meaning,
I thought it was all soppy hugs and kisses,
Followed by hollow promises and wishes,
But now you've redefined the meaning of love,
My heart yearns for you, I long for your gentle touch,
I want to hear your soothing heartbeat,
Maybe love isn't all that bad,
It is the greatest experience I've ever had
And it's all because I met you.

Darris Kiever (13)
Castle High School

An Imposter In The Family

She's coming home tomorrow,
I sit there drowning my sorrows,
An imposter, an alien invading,
I seem to be fading.

I wish this was a nightmare,
She's even taken my teddy bear,
She stole my mummy,
And even took my dummy.

She's taken my room,
So I hit her with a spoon,
They kicked me out and closed the door,
No one cares about me anymore.

At the time of dawn,
The moment she was born,
I knew it was the end for me,
This wasn't how life used to be!

Bushra Javed (13)
Castle High School

Katie

My friend Katie, she's only ten years old today,
I love it when she comes to play,
Her nana lives next door by the way,
We go swimming and the cinema too,
We have such fun in everything we do,
We are true friends and that's no lie,
We feel sad when her nana says,' Come on, say goodbye!'
But come next week, we're ready to go and do it all again,
You know we will keep all our stories and gossip too,
Till next week when I see you.

Shanaz Harris (11)
Castle High School

The Night Before Christmas

Merry Christmas to all of you
And your friends and family too,
Now, on to the poem I hope you like,
Before you ride that brand new bike.

Snowflakes falling to the ground,
Children singing all around,
Adults wrapping all the things,
That Santa Claus is going to bring,
Presents will be under the tree,
'By tomorrow,' says Mommy,
All the lights are on in the street
And everyone comes out to greet,
The sleighs are coming into sight,
But Mom says, 'For you it is goodnight!'
Stockings hanging up so high,
Just like they are in the sky,
Eyelids drooping but sleep's still far away,
Because I'm thinking of the next day.

Thoughts, of Santa's beard of snow,
What do you believe?
Ho! Ho! Ho!

Sara Wilkes (11)
Castle High School

Witches' Spell

Slimy green frogs' legs,
A big tarantula spider skewered on a peg,
Part of a pig,
A horrible mouse that was ever so big,
A fat little boy
And a broken toy,
A black and rusty bat's wing,
A giant sovereign ring.

Double, double, pop and bubble,
Fire burn and get into trouble!

Let's get ready to learn the spell,
Come and join us to learn it well,
The fin of a shark,
The stone nose of a statue at the park,
Holey clothes found at the mall,
A really dirty Adidas ball.

Double, double, pop and bubble,
Fire burn and get into trouble!
Cool it down with some sizzling snake's blood.

Bethany Higgins (12)
Castle High School

Number Eight

Number eight goes down,
He's cracked his knee!
Look at him,
Screaming out in agony.

The trainer's magic sponge,
Gets him off the deck,
The ice-cold water is
Squeezed down his neck.

He is brave and strong,
The scrum is tight,
The pack drive forward,
He is pale white.

The final whistle goes,
The team jump in the air,
They celebrate for hours,
As if they just don't care!

Shaun Thompson (11)
Castle High School

Eagle

Sweeping up high,
Diving down low,
One split second and off we go.

Accelerating speed,
A beautiful creature,
You're lucky, he might fly down to greet you.

His hunting eyes,
May be a big surprise,
When he swoops down to eat you!

Hannah-Rose Little (13)
Castle High School

Witches' Spell

Hocus pocus,
An elephant's ear,
A baby's tear,
The fresh blood of a flea,
The dirt of a key,
A kitten's nail,
A big dog's tail,
A dead vampire's blood,
A little boy's hood.

Hocus pocus,
An adult's tooth,
Add a box of Sugar Puffs,
A teacher's eye,
Add pigeon pie,
A strand of a little boy's hair,
Add a little pit of a pear,
Last but not least, a teenager's guts!

Lauren Homer (12)
Castle High School

Chocolate

C hocolate is sweet
H ow lovely it is
O h so sugary
C an be white
O r brown
L ove it forever
A nd never let go
T oo, too sweet,
E ven sweeter than you!

Jamie Guest (13)
Castle High School

Witches' Spell

A leaf from a Venus flytrap,
An Aston Villa baseball cap,
A cat's ear,
The froth of a beer
And don't forget the antlers of a deer,
Fire burning, cauldron bubbling,
Time to get our witches' spell running,
A TV remote,
A brand new Rockport coat,
A newt's tail,
A fox's tail,
The shell from a snail,
Fire burning, cauldron bubbling,
Time to get our witches' spell running,
A school tie,
A steak and kidney pie,
A lock of hair,
A claw of a bear,
The right ear from a hare
And the last ingredient, a full packet of Gaviscon
To cool it down.

John Sidwell (12)
Castle High School

The Witches' Spell

Put in the spoon,
Spin it around,
Stop when the stew is nice and brown.

Eyes of an eagle,
Tongue of a dog,
Toe of a bat,
Leg of a mouse.

Put in the spoon,
Spin it around,
Stop when the stew is nice and brown.

Creature's head, slug's slime, bat's wing,
Finger of a human man,
Hair of a little girl,
Nose of a fat man,
Stop, that's enough.

Put in the spoon,
Spin it around,
Stop when the stew is nice and brown.

Garry Allen (12)
Castle High School

Witches' Spell

Double, double, the sound of trouble,
There drops in an eye,
There falls in a brain!
Bubble, bubble, the sound of crumbling!

A pop! A pop! It's nearly finished,
A little touch of a spider . . .
A little touch of worms . . .
The ingredients are nearly vanished!

Seems like it's done . . .
But a bit more to do,
A scream full of ice cream,
That will make you dream.

Bubble, double, trouble,
Here's the end, pour it out -
A glass of wine with
A little touch of cleverness,
Ha, ha, ha, ha!

Athea Hussain (11)
Castle High School

Fashion

Fashion is my passion,
My passion is my fashion,
Mini skirts and shirts,
Looking so good it hurts,
Boots with heels,
I like the way it feels,
Curls or straight hair,
Blonde, brunette or fair,
Eyeshadow and lipgloss will suit anything,
Big earrings and diamond rings,
Eyebrows plucked and nails brightened,
Ready for a party
And looking drop dead gorgeous.

Sofia Akhtar (13)
Castle High School

Reaper's Tail

Hocus, pocus, rats and bats,
Join us in this spell of cats,
Witches on their broomsticks arrive,
To conjure a spell that will cast out lives,
Potions of red and blue liquids,
Beginning to bubble in a boiling pot.

Hocus, pocus, rats and bats,
The rituals begin,
Casting out the evil sins,
Circle round witches as the
Bubbles begin to jump,
Casting out the eyes of cats about.

Hocus, pocus, the deed is done,
Now my spell has come to an end,
The stars are bright and
The moon is high, so let's hope
There are no more witches in the sky.

Richard Holness (12)
Castle High School

Christmas Morning

I wake up really early, excitement in my head,
Although it's still dark, I spring out of bed,
I'm down the stairs and through the door,
I just can't wait to go and explore,
I look around and what do I see?
Bags full of presents - and all for me!
I jump to the floor and what do I see?
A BMX and lots of money, all for me,
I feel like a millionaire, but not quite there,
But there's more than enough for me,
So I don't care!

Jake Taylor (11)
Castle High School

Love Is?

Love is like a flower,
It grows within time,
More and more beautiful,
Watching it shine.

Love is like a rain shower,
Suddenly flows upon you,
When you least expect it,
Comes out of the blue.

Love is like a fire,
It confuses your mind,
But sometimes it burns out
And doesn't seem so kind.

Love is like pain,
A knife stabbing into your heart,
If it doesn't go right,
Then why did it ever start?

But love is a great thing
And true love is rare,
It should be treasured,
It's the best thing to share.

Katie Louise Willis (13)
Castle High School

Bubble, Bubble

A snail's shell
And a large whale's fin,
Let the cauldron start bubbling . . .
Bubble, bubble, let's start trouble!

A giant's leg
And cat's fur,
A frog's tongue with gory blood on top . . .
Bubble, bubble, let's start trouble!

A few wriggly worms
And a hippo's germs
And a pig's eye wrapped in foil . . .
Bubble, bubble, let's start trouble!

A human heart
And a big smelly fart,
Mix the potion and say . . .
Bubble, bubble, let's start trouble!

A lion's mane
And a small toy plane,
A camel's hump . . .
Bubble, bubble, let's start trouble!

Iram Ilyas (12)
Castle High School

The Cauldron

Gather round and hear my spell,
Say it loud and learn it well,
Put the ingredients into the pot,
Stir it well until it's hot.

Eye of cat and tail of fog,
Wing of a bat and rotting frog.

Throw in a rock star's finger,
We throw in Jerry Springer.

Eye of a tiger,
In goes Maguer.

In goes eye of newt,
Woman goes down the garbage shoot.

Blood of witch and neck of goose,
Twist its head until it's loose.

Gather round and hear my spell,
Say it loud and learn it well,
Put the ingredients into the pot,
Stir it well until it's hot.

James Baker (12)
Castle High School

The Witches' Spell

A rat's tail,
A slimy snail,
A bottle of rum,
A big thumb,
A fat little boy,
A half-broken toy,
The rattle of a rattlesnake
And a marmalade cake.

We will kindle the fire,
We are alive,
We are alive,
As the Earth is alive,
We have the power to
Create our freedom.

A silver ghost,
A piece of burnt toast,
An alive chicken
And a mushy pea tin,
A big fat dragon,
A big black cannon,
Two boxes of chilli,
The seeds of a lily.

Alcaash Mahroof (12)
Castle High School

Spell

(Inspired by Macbeth)

Witches' fiddle, turnip middle,
Scoop it all out with a spoon,
Curve of mouth and eyes,
With a carving knife,
Beneath a Hallowe'en moon.

'We are a circle,
We are a circle,
With no beginning and no ending'.

Witch's broom, handle long, wax candle,
Stick spell firm in the hole,
Find a moth, step back and watch.

'We are a circle,
We are a circle,
With no beginning and no ending'.

A rat's tail, a hairy whale,
Wool off a bat, fur off a cat,
Armpit hair, a grizzly bear,
For a charm of powerful trouble,
Like a hell-broth boil and bubble.

Emily Reed (12)
Castle High School

The Sky

It was a beautiful spring morning and the sky was blue
And when I looked up at it, it had the same colour eyes as you,
You were in the next bedroom,
As I kept peeping through,
I went and sat on your bed
And I put my hand on your delicate head,
I put the breakfast on the floor
And after that I went to my bedroom door
And I went back to bed,
Later on,
I woke up on the floor
And I heard the door,
I ran to the window, it was you,
With suitcases in your hand,
I shouted out your name,
But you did not hear
And as the time passed by,
A tear came from my eye,
I started to cry for you,
That's why I said the sky is always grey,
Without you.

Bianca Bell (12)
Castle High School

Witches' Cauldron

(Inspired by Macbeth)

'Double, double, toil and trouble,
Fire burn and cauldron bubble'.
Eye of a newt and tongue of dog,
A rat's tail and meat of hog,
Mix it up with all your might,
Or you will have a terrible fright,
'Double, double, toil and trouble,
Fire burn and cauldron bubble'.
A wasp's nest and a poison ivy sting,
An elephant's nose and rotten steak pie,
An adder's fork and a flea's eye,
'Double, double, toil and trouble,
Fire burn and cauldron bubble'.
Guts of goat and rotten honey,
Dog's tooth and lots of money,
Rabbits' whiskers and eye of a cat,
Into the cauldron and that is that,
'Double, double, toil and trouble,
Fire burn and cauldron bubble'.

Reece Wainwright (12)
Castle High School

The Phoenix

Light blazing,
Across the sky,
Enormous creature
Appears from the ground.

Invisible
And back again after 500 yeas,
Me and you,
Don't know his origin,
Mythical creature.

Golden wings,
Spread out,
Filling the sky,
Size of an eagle,
Gold plumage neck,
Purple body,
Azure tail.

Dies in a blaze of fire
And back again!

Aneesah Sagir (14)
Castle High School

Bubbling Boils

Gather round and hear my spell,
A rat's tail
And a slimy snail,
Start the cauldron bubbling,
Bubble, bubble, boiling boils . . .

Purr of a cat,
Wing of a bat,
Keep that cauldron bubbling,
Bubble, bubble, boiling boils . . .

Spiders, snakes,
Those things too
And maybe even monkey poo,
The cauldron keeps bubbling,
Bubble, bubble, boiling boils . . .

Moths' wings, you know, those things,
Bulls' horns and
Roses' thorns,
Keep that cauldron bubbling,
Bubble, bubble, boiling boils . . .

A rotten pear
And a schoolgirl's hair . . . Do you care?
That cauldron keeps bubbling,
Bubble, bubble, boiling boils . . .

A boy's boil
And a pig's eye covered in tin foil,
Stir it all up,
Have a taste . . . *mmmm* . . . this tastes great,
Bubble, bubble, boiling boils.

Emma Louise Bibb (12)
Castle High School

The Snake

Like a teenager on holiday,
It crouches in wait,
On rocks, soaking up the heat.
Like an arrow from its lair,
It shoots and plunges,
Its stiletto fangs,
Into unsuspecting victims,
With poison like syrup,
Thick and fatal.
Its eyes like glowing rubies,
Set back and mysterious,
Surrounded by scales,
Like tiny shimmering jewels,
Like rainbows trapped in bubbles.
The snake;
Beautiful and deadly.

Sarah Battye (12)
Codsall Middle School

Funky Fabulous

High heels, make-up and mascara,
My gorgeous dress and my gold tiara,
Wavy hair and luscious lips,
All the girls shaking their hips,
All the boys bobbing up and down,
The disc in the player going round and round,
Bright red nails and a diamond ring,
That's my sister with all that bling,
Smelling like roses
And doing lots of poses,
The boys are tying to dance,
But are really pants,
I don't care what you say,
I'm going to dance the night away!

Kirsty Howat (11)
Codsall Middle School

The Best Friend Poem

They're always there for you,
Like they could be your shadow,
You couldn't live without them,
Like they're an important part of your body,
You can trust them with any secret
And they will keep it locked up inside them,
They will always listen to what you're saying,
Like an extra pair of ears,
They know what you're thinking,
Like a clone of you,
They are hard to find,
Like the perfect pair of shoes,
You get closer to them by day,
As the sun gets hotter,
They will always be supportive,
Close to your heart and aren't easy to find,
Like a brilliant bra!

Sally Cassandra Smallman (13)
Codsall Middle School

Ivy Cottage

Like a royal garden,
The hanging baskets drape down,
Like a snake after its prey,
The ivy climbs to find sunlight,
The pretty thatched roof,
Like a hurricane of straw has occurred,
The big old front door,
Like an entrance to an ogre's castle,
The juicy vegetable patch,
Like a hungry rabbit's heaven,
Mouth-watering, jaw-dropping smell,
Like a sweet sugary bakery,
Ivy Cottage,
Like a paradise in the countryside,
Like an unreal painting,
Like a flower ready to blossom.

Georgina Christie (13)
Codsall Middle School

The Pumpkin Poem

There was a woman dressed in pink,
To strangers she was Mrs Twink,
She had a pumpkin with a long green stalk,
But it was different, it could talk!

Till one day she took her knife,
She was going to take the pumpkin's life,
The pumpkin shouted in alarm,
'Please don't take my arm!'
'You don't have arms!' the woman cried,
She stabbed the pumpkin, then it died.

She didn't give it a funeral though,
She put it on the red-hot shove,
Now what was the point of that?
Instead she should have stewed her cat,
Then she would have had some meat,
Because pumpkin's are not that good to eat.

Natalie Bosworth (11)
Codsall Middle School

Dear God

Dear God,
I would like to know . . .
Why does everybody fight
And say that they are right?

Why is everyone in pain,
Even though the saying is 'No pain, no gain'?
Why does everybody starve?

And in other parts of the world they're rich enough to buy cars?
Why does everybody thirst
And other people drink so much water?
They feel like their tummies will burst.

Why aren't people allowed to learn
And other people aren't even concerned?
Please answer my questions when I pray
And hopefully that will be today.

Isabelle Bates (11)
Codsall Middle School

My Family

My brother eats and eats,
My sisters hate all meats,
My mom is a clean freak,
My dad is extremely bleak,
My sisters have long hair,
My brother eats like a bear,
My brother smells like eggs,
My mom does the washing with pegs,
My dog is oh so skinny,
My cat's name is Vinny,
My mom's overprotective,
My sister's no detective,
My brother likes football,
My pet spider lives in the hall,
My brother eats and eats,
My sisters hate all meats,
My mom is a clean freak,
My dad is extremely bleak,
Whereas I am perfect.

Jacob Laybourne (13)
Codsall Middle School

The Sea

The waves roar like a lion,
Boats like tiny crabs sit silently waiting,
The sun reflecting like a mirror,
Blue like the sky,
The wind whistles like a bird,
The land beyond like a tiny island lost forever,
Foam-like white horses galloping.

Sophie Yates (12)
Codsall Middle School

Aliens

Long tentacle-like whips,
Inside eyes like black slits,
Blood like acid steaming,
Laser guns like bright lights beaming,
Head like a round melon,
They killed a man, his name was Lennon,
Their ship like a flying plate,
Using their minds to meditate,
Sharp teeth like samurai's,
Looking out for predators with their eyes,
Eating people's heads off all the time
And for their drink, they have some wine,
Interior like a shopping mall,
Once you're in it's like a barricaded wall,
Their blood-sucking alien things,
Destroying anything that their people bring.

Alex Burgess (12)
Codsall Middle School

In His Arms

There she lay,
By Summer Bay,
She daydreamed of his love and his good charms,
She would come to no harm,
Lying in his arms.

Their kiss was soft,
Like the flutter of a moth,
With all his care,
He stroked her hair,
They signified their love in open air,
To show the world they didn't care.

Emily Humphreys (12)
Edgecliff High School

A Thunderstorm Is . . .

A scary face,
A sad painting,
A dangerous place,
Death waiting.

A firework display,
A power cut,
A game to play,
A stamping foot.

A loud drum roll,
A vicious fight,
A big black hole,
An amazing sight.

A witch's spell,
An army of guns,
A punishment from Hell,
One of Dad's bad puns.

In a thunderstorm, what do you see?
Opinions change between you and me,
For some it's a wonderful place to be,
For others, it will never ever be.

Cerys Mabe (13)
Edgecliff High School

Clouds On The Night Sky

As they pass by on their never-ending crusade,
Like a leaf on a lake, no control where they go,
Seeing everything in the world with a hawk's-eye scope,
Able to cloak the moon with a whisper of the wind.

Some may stop to gaze upon all that Man has made,
Upon a brilliant cyan sky this shining white avalanche flows,
All the time we are at war they can cope,
Never are they in the same place, or on a spot pinned.

Some say the dead do not die, but are caught,
Able to watch their heirs, grief and mirth,
I believe they travel in the clouds of the mid-way Heaven, like these,
Following the currents and seeing both mirth and melancholy,
They see Man both in confidence,
A change of wind and see Man trembling on its knees,
Forever and eternity, mid-Heaven is where you see Man
Come and go, on the Earth.

Josef Baker (12)
Edgecliff High School

Nature

I love watching the trees
They swing and sway in the breeze.

The squirrels jump and scurry,
Without any worry,
Gathering the nuts and seeds.

So listen to the lovely breeze,
To calm yourself
And let nature breed,
Come and see the sight as wonderful as it is.

Charlotte Tustin (11)
George Salter High School

Feelings

I have felt many feelings before,
The worst was when we split and tore,
I know that I never show you,
But my love for you is ever true,
Please, I am begging, don't leave me this way,
Please can we try again from yesterday?
I know I'm not great, nowhere near perfect,
I really should show you more respect;
You are my star,
You are my light,
You were the girl I kissed goodnight,
But now all you say is 'Get out of my sight'.

Girl my love for you, will never end,
Enough, you don't even see me as a friend,
I know that it is my entire fault
And now my life has come to a very sharp halt,
I miss you, I swear it's true
And in my life there is always space for you.

Liam Johnson (15)
George Salter High School

Away With Words

The boats crashed on the beach,
The men charged for their lives,
There was no chance they would reach,
But they had to try and survive.

The enemies were grinning with glee,
Their sergeant was barking, 'Kill the enemy!'
Thinking to themselves, *How hard could this be?*
The only way to find out was to wait and see.

The Allies moved forward in unison,
Under artillery cover,
Their lieutenant did order, 'Shoot them son,'
The soldiers could only think of their lonely lovers.

There was a deep rumbling sound,
A shout of sympathy,
The soldiers of the Axis, lying on the ground,
Their lives have changed, but they are forever free.

Away with words.

Grant Banner (15)
George Salter High School

Away With Words

The flick of a page,
A sudden trigger of emotions,
The continuous literature
A library of apparitions,
The dance of the imagination,
A chorus of exhilarating lines,
The influence of the mind,
An art scattered through the letters,
The entrance behind the thought
The ambiguity of the author,
The genre of all ages,
The sequel edition soon behind,
Many personal judgements,
Only the single ending,
The numerous drafts,
An unexpected character,
The tense moments,
A sudden romance,
The stir of the make-believe world,
A coma within the book,
A rush of fulfilment,
The final sentence,
The ultimate dot,
A finished version,
The delight of the author.

Adeela Waid (15)
George Salter High School

George Salter High School

George Salter High School,
Is my school,
When I walked through the doors,
I thought I would come back,
With bruises and sores,
When I strolled through the hall,
I saw the children wide and tall
And thought I was the only one that was small,
But when I found my friends,
That's when the scariness started to end
And I like my teachers,
Especially my English teacher,
She is really cool,
Now I love going to school,
I've got all the support I need,
I like it here, yes indeed,
I feel really safe and secure,
Much better than I did before,
It turned out I didn't have bruises and sores,
I know I am OK because,
George Salter High School,
Is my school.

Sherilyn Gwen Smith (11)
George Salter High School

Away With Words

I sit here alone
And away with words,
Each letter curves
Lingering still,
Now renting the
Empty space within my mind.

Being away with words,
Is like being away from sound,
That once made a soft smile,
Play around my lips.

Now my face has no expression,
Looking back at by broken reflection,
Haunting the image that there once was.

I now sit here alone,
Away with words,
Away from sound,
Away from home.

Sarah Cumberlidge (15)
George Salter High School

Away With Words

As I shut the curtain
And lay down my head,
Words blow me away.

As I shut my eyes
And dream with words,
Does it matter what I say?

When you run away with what I say,
Along with my soul which you stole,
Just, from speaking a word,
Clipping what was whole.

When I open my eyes
And undroop my head,
The wind served to blow.

When I open the curtains
And see my life
And not this dream I know

Who I am.

John Richards (15)
George Salter High School

Away With Words

At the start we were great,
Always together, day in, day out,
It was all love, never hate,
I loved you so much, I just wanted to shout.

A few months down the line,
Everyone knew that we were going strong,
I was all yours, and you were all mine,
We both felt this relationship was going to last long.

Wow, we've lasted a whole year,
For me it's been nothing but smiles,
Every day I told you I'd always be here,
Deep down inside, I knew we could go for miles.

Then there was that month we weren't so strong,
You sat me down for that dreaded talk,
All I wanted to know was what had gone wrong,
Then it was obvious it was time to walk.

You just left me standing there,
My heart completely split into thirds,
I really thought we were a perfect pair,
But no, now I'm just away with words.

Christopher Griffin (15)
George Salter High School

Away With Words

The wooden box,
Coming closer towards my eye,
I go in,
The tight cramped space of the confessional box,
Compacts the bones in my body.

'Forgive me Lord for I have sinned,'
I say whilst sitting in this wooden bin,
Away with words, away with words.

I throw away my darkest sin,
Like rubbish falling in this wooden bin,
Away with words, away with words.

The wooden box,
Now disappearing from eyes of mine,
I walk away,
Knowing that tomorrow, again I will pray,
I wish to be free, free like a bird,
But only if I'm away with words.
Away from words,
Away from sin.

Jak Garrity (15)
George Salter High School

Away With Words

The valley of the dead,
Where endless blood is shed
And tireless children, forced to fight,
Witness hopeful parents lose their heads.

Endless wars and lifelong battles,
Between the arrogant and their offspring,
When the battle is won and the dead are buried,
The victorious shall crown themselves king.

Not one side will apologise
And put this war to an end,
So the hateful, arrogant foes attack
And the faithful are forced to defend.

The constant slaughter and limbs being torn,
Makes all live in fear,
You see this world and wish you weren't born
And all are forced to shed a tear.

Daniel McDonald (15)
George Salter High School

Away With Words

My loving family,
My family cares about me,
When I'm feeling down or lonely,
They're always there for me like a big family tree,
I love them and they love me, for them I am always free.
My dad is special as can be,
My mum is caring just like me,
To me my family is like a heart of love and to them
I am a cute little white dove,
My sisters are clever just like me
And my brother is a busy bee,
My family is special in every way,
I'll keep on loving them every day.

Babley Zaman (11)
George Salter High School

Away With Words

Don't say anything,
Don't be absurd,
Actions speak louder,
Away with words.

Look into my eyes,
What do you see?
I see you
And you see me.

Your gentle touch,
Drives me mad,
But when you're away,
It makes me sad.

I know your mind,
Like my own,
But when I'm by myself,
I'm never alone.

Don't say anything,
Don't be absurd,
Actions speak louder,
Away with words.

Sonia Nath (15)
George Salter High School

Why Me!

Angry, annoyed, frustrated,
Why, why was it me?
Why did I get caught?
It takes two to tango
And two to talk
And why am I wasting
My time when it was
Someone else's fault?

Catherine Coakley (14)
Hagley RC High School

Child Abuse

Screams of children coming from next door,
The worries of hurt racing through my mind,
He comes home, angry and depressed,
Goes up to them and soothes his anger,
By hitting them.
Happiness does not exist in their lives,
Only sorrow and sadness,
Wishing, hoping it will end,
Trying to smile while hiding the bruises,
The pain must be unbearable,
They fear their own father,
He haunts them in their nightmares,
Too frightened to scream, '*Stop!*'

Katie Conlon (14)
Hagley RC High School

It's Not Fair

He picks on me every time,
I wasn't the one talking,
'Detention' he shouts down the class to me,
'This lunch, if you don't turn up after school.'
She was talking to me,
I never said anything.
Sat in the detention wasting my time,
For something I didn't do,
Steam coming out of my ears,
I felt like a train,
Getting angry more each time he shouted,
'Never talk again.'
'I didn't do anything!'

Jennifer Barry (13)
Hagley RC High School

That Freaky Kid

They bawl out 'Monkey' and 'Spade'
And the anger and resentment fills him up,
Like a violent crater about to blow,
A memory flashes through his absent mind,
There is just a boy, shivering on his own,
In a solitary and desolate corner,
A teardrop here, a sniffle there,
Not welcome at home, or at the schoolyard,
That freaky kid who sits by himself,
Afraid to talk, the colour of his ancestors,
Has turned him into a social outcast,
His turban is stained and ripped,
He glances up, only to see a fist,
Approaching his cut, bruised face.

Greg Humphries (13)
Hagley RC High School

Goodbye

I'm scared of letting people in,
I'm scared of being hurt,
Not sure how to get through this,
Don't know how I should feel.
Because when you died,
I couldn't believe it was real,
Don't think I can trust people,
Why did you have to go?
I feel so lost and empty,
Now you're six feet under
And guess what? I can't bring you back,
You're gone and I can't deal with that.

Whitney Rowles
Hagley RC High School

Terror

London,
The capital city
Centre of terrorists.

Taking a step underground,
Shuffling along the platform,
Carried into the carriage,
Wishing you weren't there,
Gripping the handle, scanning the dull walls,
Imagining that day over and over,
The bombings,
The people.

Robyn Brooks
Hagley RC High School

Goodbye

What a waste,
Never fulfilled all of life,
Such a tender age,
It makes me so angry, in such a rage.
Why is evil saved,
But good sacrificed?
Goodbye, goodnight, lay your head,
You may be dead as some say,
Goodnight for now until another day.

Daniel Cullen (13)
Hagley RC High School

Injustice

Afghanistan, Iraq, war over there,
Bush and Blair just don't care,
War is bringing injustice and hate,
Races are being separated, we all should be mates.

Just think of the people dying,
Disease and dirt, a baby crying,
All this war is affecting us in Britain you see,
Being a Muslim seems a bad person to be.

Danny Cameron (14)
Hagley RC High School

Great World War

Pain, destruction, death, despair,
The war is coming, be ready, beware,
Is there any love? Can there be any cheer,
When all the nations of the Earth come crashing down?
How can there be safety?
How can there be joy
If the governments are in such turmoil?
Look at the world around you,
Look at the children playing,
Look at the people you know,
Now they're here, now they're gone,
How long shall we be in darkness?
How long shall we be afraid?
Pain, destruction, death, despair,
The war is coming, be ready, beware.

The world of fear
The world of war.

George Meadows (13)
Henley-in-Arden High School

Who Would Do This To A Homeless Child?

I open my eyes, I can't hear a sound,
I'm sitting here alone on the dirty ground,
Not one human in my sight,
The only thing I want is to get rid of this fright.

I'm cold, I'm tired,
I never seem to sleep,
If I do my belongings never seem to keep,
They just disappear in the middle of the night,
When I wake there's nothing in sight,
My blanket's gone as well as my coat,
Who would do this to a homeless child?

To do something like this, they must be sad,
What does it do, make them glad?
It makes me sad but I don't know why,
Why would they do this to a homeless child?

I have no family,
I have no home,
All I have is myself all alone.

I wish my sadness would just disappear,
I wish my head would just give up and clear.

Why do these people let us live like this,
All we have is one single wish,
'We wish we were happy',
That's all we want, including myself,
So please stop this and please just help!
Who would do this to a homeless child?

Katie Sheridan (13)
Henley-in-Arden High School

There's Always A Result In The End!

I twizzle, I turn, I try my best,
I can't get it right, and I need a rest,
My hands are blistered, and my feet are bruised,
But I am so determined not to lose.

My heart is thumping, my stomach has butterflies,
It just gets worse when the crowd screams and cries,
My nerves are tense,
As my opponent starts and presents.

Her performance is pretty perfect,
Definitely a routine I shouldn't neglect,
Nine point two is her score,
That means I have to get more.

All is quiet as I walk onto the floor,
Everyone's watching and that's for sure,
When I am finished, the crowd is cheering,
I can't believe what I am hearing.

Oh my lord, I've got nine point seven,
I feel like I am up in Heaven,
We're waiting for the names to be called out,
I'm first, I just want to dance, scream and shout.

Giving up is incorrect,
I work and work till it is perfect,
There is always something to tidy or mend,
But there is always a result in the end.

Caroline Curry (13)
Henley-in-Arden High School

What If . . . ?

What if I could turn back time . . .
Would I change a thing?
Would I mend my mistakes
Or keep life as it is?

What if I could?
Would I try a little harder at my tests,
Receive a bright gold sticker
And be the teacher's pet?

Would I change the day,
My skirt caught on the gate,
Bright pink knickers flashing,
Everybody laughing at my fate?

Maybe I would turn back time,
To when terror began,
Make sure war never happened
And people could live again.

Or would I go back to
The day I lost my running race,
I could run a little faster
And keep a steady pace?

What if I could go back to
The day my granny died?
We were warned so I was going to play a special tune,
But we were not on time.

Life does funny things to you,
Some are hard to take,
But take these times and use them,
To learn from your mistakes.

Even if I could change the past,
I'm not so sure I would,
For all things I've come across,
Have taught me what is good.

Nobody is perfect,
Just look around and you will see,
Everybody does things wrong,
Even counting me!

Becky Gee **(13)**
Henley-in-Arden High School

Love

I sit alone in the darkness,
Waiting,
Waiting for him to come to me.

Can he hear my cries?
Can he feel my tears?
Can he sense my breaking heart?
He himself only knows the facts.

Where did I go wrong?
How can this be that he can't see?
Is it because I'm alone in the dark?
I just walk past as if I am invisible.

Can he see me now?
Can he see the pain he's caused me,
Or does he just look past it?
Is this a dream or true life?

I think I should move on,
But something tells me to wait,
My heart,
He needs to prove his love to me.

As I return to sit alone in the dark,
Waiting,
Waiting for his love.

Shaun Parsons **(13)**
Henley-in-Arden High School

America Poem

I had the perfect life,
I had all I could need,
All I wanted was already there,
So there never was a need to plead.

I had a ton of friends,
Who accepted me for who I am,
My favourite friend was Hannah,
My favourite dog was Sam.

I also loved my house,
It was big and very cool,
We had a huge backyard,
Which also contained a pool.

I especially loved my school,
I would never be the one to tease,
I loved all of my teachers
And I could wear whatever I pleased.

Then I had to move,
To a space so far away,
We all started crying,
Because we could no longer play.

Things are so different here,
I feel like I don't fit in,
We have to wear uniforms
And sometimes it feels like my accent's a sin.

Now I live in England,
Next to Paris, Spain and Rome,
I'm not sure if I like it here,
I think I prefer it more at home.

Alex Stimpson (13)
Henley-in-Arden High School

Will You?

You're all I've ever wanted,
Without you I just couldn't cope,
In this crazy world we live in,
You're my life, my love, my hope.

As I sail through this,
Troublesome thing called life,
I wonder deeply,
How I became your wife.

I remember we walked,
Along Blackpool pier,
Romantic love songs,
Is all I could hear.

It's been nine months,
Since we met on that hot summer day,
Our love blossomed
And never faltered to this day.

Then in May 2006,
You got down on one knee,
Popped that special question
And waited to find out and see.

Of course
I said yes,
How could I
Have said anything less.

You're all I've ever wanted,
Without you I just couldn't cope.

Hannah Roberts (13)
Henley-in-Arden High School

Us Kids

Us kids, we're always getting done,
Told off for everything, even having fun,
Hanging around the sidewalk, doing nothing wrong,
People think we're up to something, they think we're there too long.

We're accused, we're shouted at, we're told we're a waste of space,
We can never just relax, 'cause they're always on our case,
Moaning, groaning sad old ladies with nothing better to do,
They stand up in their kitchen windows and point their fingers at you.

But now my teenage childhood is coming to an end,
No more moaning, groaning neighbours to drive me around the bend,
'Cause I'll be out at work all day, keeping myself busy,
It'll be all the other lads, driving the old women dizzy.

Ryan Harvey (13)
Henley-in-Arden High School

Work Life

Drain and pillage from your vivid eyes,
Store them away when the alarm clock rings,
Cleanse your joyous face of the conflict inside,
Tedious labour is calling with venom lure,
The weary day has awoken once more,
Shed identity and talent from this world,
Immerse yourself in their grey logical life,
You have no individuality or thought,
Become a minute member of an infinite crowd
And drag your fatigued body to your empty desk,
Sit and write like your co-workers are,
Stare in a mirror at your panic-gripped, pasty face,
But don't be original, look the same, like everyone else.

George Wilson (13)
Henley-in-Arden High School

The Little Red Rose

The little red rose swayed in the breeze,
The wind rustled through the trees,
Oh yes, yes, yes, what lovely weather,
Thought the little red rose,
Amongst the clumps of heather,
A sweet-smelling scent of thick, golden honey,
Wafted from the trees,
It did smell yummy,
No one ever smiled at the little red rose,
Because she was so grumpy and stuck up her nose,
Then one day the little red rose made
A big mistake that changed her ways,
Instead of putting on her bright red shades,
She put on those of her great aunt Petalade,
She did look silly in that blue and yellow pair,
To all the other flowers,
She gave quite a scare,
The little red rose was very shocked to see,
All the other flowers smile at her with glee!
All the baby flowers laughed to see her face,
Instead of looking at her with hatred and disgrace,
After that one day,
The red rose learnt to smile
And to her pleasant surprise,
She found it quite worthwhile
And also after that, new friends the red rose made,
But all thanks to
Her great aunt Petalade!

Emily Hancock (11)
Henley-in-Arden High School

National Schools' Trampolining Champion 2003

Competition today, I can feel the nerves,
I feel so weird inside,
All the what ifs are pushed to the back of my mind,
My worries which I can't confide.

Keep telling myself *by tonight it'll be over,*
Just to concentrate on the task at hand,
Can't forget about the slight bit of doubt,
To try my best is what I demand.

I think that if I try my best,
Even if I messed up or fell,
At least I wouldn't feel guilty after,
My pride I won't be able to sell.

I sit in the corner of a crowded room
And think of what my coaches told me,
Hold your arms, and point your toes,
As if it is them who I can see.

I get on and present to the judges,
The first move out of the way,
The rest of the routine is easy from now,
I want this moment to forever stay.

I finish the routine very well
And the judges give me a high score,
The next routine goes better than the last,
All the competitors stare in awe.

My coach comes over with a grin on her face,
She spins me around and around,
She tells me I am British Schools' Champion 2003,
I've done it, I really have, the bounty I have found.

Elizabeth Hansen (14)
Henley-in-Arden High School

What Is The World?

Do you ever question,
What your purpose is in life?
So many questions to be asked,
Answers that you can wonder.

Have you ever thought,
What the world is all about?
Is it money, survival or something else,
Like friendship, peace and love?

Do you sit and watch,
The seasons roll on by?
Red and gold leaves raining down,
The bright sunshine warming the world.

Do you ever stop and think,
That each of us is special?
Are our lives already planned out
Or is our future unknown by anyone?

Do you ever ponder the thought,
That the world is an age-old mystery?
Was it formed from religion or from science instead?
The beginning of our creation unknown to mankind.

Have you ever really noticed,
Why the roses are red and the sky is blue?
Why friendships are made but memories fade?
These are but a few of the mysteries of life. ,

So have you reached a final conclusion,
About the mysterious meaning of life,
Or will we simply never know the truth,
To a question from the dawn of time?

Eleanor Wilson (13)
Henley-in-Arden High School

I Have Words But Cannot Speak

I have words but cannot speak,
I am a creature, cruelly treated,
My owners abused me,
Treated me like dirt.

I had four legs,
But due to neglect I have three,
I was thin and weak
And had to scavenge for food.

But now I have new owners,
A young loving family,
I have food and water
And a comfy bed.

Children play with me,
They throw me sticks to hobble after,
They are kind to me
And my life is easy.

Life is great,
I can lie out in the sun,
In my brightly coloured room,
Without a worry in the world.

As I compare life to what it was,
I got it easy in the end,
Since I ran away,
But I still have words and cannot speak.

James Elliott (13)
Henley-in-Arden High School

Inside These Four Walls . . .

Inside these four walls,
Is where all the laughter falls,
No one can help me, no one can see,
Just what they're really doing to me.

I cry, I scream, I shout, I yelp,
Just for anyone, the tiniest bit of help,
People walk by me, they see me, they stare,
Not knowing what's going on, not even a care.

The bruises, the scars, they'll be there till the end,
Haunting me from my past, like a ghostly fiend,
It's all their fault but no one realises,
Just how truly horrible my life is.

I can't escape even though I try,
No matter how much I cry,
All I want is a new beginning,
All I want is a reason for living.

I don't understand . . . what have I done?
They used to tell me I was their world, their moon, their sun,
But now they constantly hit me, there is no end,
If only it was easy for a heart to mend.

They play happy families, pretending it's going to be OK,
'Tell anyone and we'll hurt you,' that's what they say,
If only they knew the pain that was caused,
As I sit inside these four walls.

Lauren Haslam (13)
Henley-in-Arden High School

We Look Happy, Us Three, Behind Closed Doors, If Only They Could See!

Why can't my parents see,
What is really wrong with me?

I couldn't take it for another month,
Stuck inside her, being her bump!

I'm not a bump; I'm a little baby,
Would they love me? It's a maybe!

No kisses, smiles or a hug,
They scream and shout, blood splatters the rug!

They obviously don't know what I need,
Not a smack, maybe just a feed!

To be parents, they are not fit,
Well they certainly aren't making a good job of it!

As I grow, I learn more and more,
I cry as Daddy shoves Mummy to the wall!

When we are out we look happy, us three,
Behind closed doors, if only they could see!

I wish that I could scream and shout,
I wish someone would come and get me,
Anyone who could help!

Physically abusing me, all of that pain,
What did I ever do to them? What do they have to gain?

To them I am just a stupid baby,
I know they don't love me, it's not even a maybe!

Kayleigh Bradley (14)
Henley-in-Arden High School

Tinky

(In loving memory of Tinky)

When I first saw your face,
Your tiny furry paws,
Your jet-black curls so soft,
Your perfect shiny claws.

You ran across the garden,
Barking as you flew,
Like angels up in Heaven,
There was just me and you.

Your toys were all around,
Your trowel of vivid green,
Yards of toys been dropped around,
Were all that could be seen.

Walkies were the best of times,
We took you off your lead,
You went trotting up the hill,
Until you couldn't be seen.

When Chloe would come with old Sam,
You'd play for hours on end,
You would stand under good Sam,
As if it were a trend.

But soon did Sam go away,
Never to be seen,
Your twinkling tiny eyes,
Did now not even gleam.

Now you're gone to Heaven
And having fun up high,
Now you are an angel
And I'm trying not to cry.

Katie Brinkworth (13)
Henley-in-Arden High School

Childhood Memories

When I was little,
Everything was different,
We used to spend all day outside,
Not worrying about being taken or harmed,
Now we have to be back before it gets dark
And tell our parents where we are.

So instead we play on the computer,
Or perhaps watch the game on TV
And still manage to gobble down a massive truckload of tea!
Now if we were outside,
Playing in the park,
We'd come home and have tea,
Then hurry back to the park
And play ponies or tag until it got dark!

We'd rush back for our supper,
Then a story by the fire,
Brush our teeth, get ready for bed,
We've another early start!
Back to the park the next day,
Again 'til it gets dark!

Now don't you just wish,
You could relive,
All your childhood memories?

Daisy Smith (13)
Henley-in-Arden High School

The World Keeps Turning

Everybody knows the world keeps turning,
Ignorance runs high, with no life learning,
Everybody has those dark, depressing days,
When it seems like your world starts to fray.
It's a shock when it comes to it,
One day you'll see,
There are people far worse off than you and me.
You're sitting at the table, drinking your fine wine,
Yet someone in the world isn't having such a good time,
This poem is not to guilt, nor is it to shame,
This world keeps turning, forever the same,
It's a shock when it comes to it,
One day you'll see,
There are people far worse off than you and me.
Everybody knows the world keeps turning,
The ignorance runs high, with no life learning.

Chloe Harrison (13)
Henley-in-Arden High School

The Homeless Animal

I am a poor homeless animal, out on the streets,
With nowhere much to go,
No more happy family to play with and love.
No heat or warmth,
Just cardboard boxes and newspapers and rubbish all around.
So this is where I have to live and hopefully I will be found.

When you are living out on the street, nothing is the same,
The food is disgusting and isn't like it was,
No bones or treats and that is just not right,
So when you decide to get a pet, think very carefully,
Don't let the poor thing end up like me!

Amey Walker (13)
Henley-in-Arden High School

Climbing Everest

A giant mass of rock-solid stone,
As tall as the eye can see,
A huge giant feat to try and accomplish,
Even if you are as skilled as me,
I look over to Tenzing Norgay,
He'll be my partner in crime for now,
We'll climb it together all day and all night,
Even if I don't know how.

It started way back almost three years ago,
Oh how the time flies by,
When we were training for those long months,
All the time but why?
We had just one goal, a suitable aim,
We knew after this, our lives would not be the same.

We practised on mountains all over the country,
Learning and training up hard,
Until that day came when we both had to go,
Packing away good luck cards,
We were putting our lives at risk you see,
While attempting this climb,
But I'd do it again as the exhilaration is,
So completely and utterly divine.

The work and the effort really was hard,
Climbing up a straight rock face,
When we reached the top and looked all around,
Things all fell into place,
I left my own message right there in the snow,
All the way at the top,
I buried a pencil, a toy cat, some sweets
And left them all at the top.

The long journey down passed without incident,
We were all happy with what we had done,
But if we thought that it was all over then,
We were wrong, it all had just begun,
So here I am living in luxury,
Knowing that I accomplished my aim,
I am working to show that the environment
Should be respected and treated well,
Life is a chance not just a game.

Emily Allen (13)
Henley-in-Arden High School

Nobody's Child

I stare out of the window,
I think of a person,
I think of a place,
I wish I were there.

The page in front of me,
Filled with meaningless words,
Somewhere in there is the key,
To my past and my future.

People come and go,
But no one stays,
No friends or foe,
It's as if I am invisible.

The horrors the night brings,
I hug myself tight,
I listen carefully as the nightingale sings,
For that is my only pleasure in life.

No one cares about a lowly orphan,
No mother or father,
No brother or sister,
Just me . . .

Zoë Gardner (13)
Henley-in-Arden High School

Our Children

What has become of our children?
Always being blamed for crimes,
What has become of our children?
What's happened to their lives?

What has become of our children?
Doing graffiti when they can,
What has become of our children?
Getting drunk every night.

What has become of our children?
Misbehaving at school,
What has become of our children?
Disrupting our community.

What has become of our children?
Coming home late at night,
What has become of our children?
Are they ever going to be right?

Matt Holtom (13)
Henley-in-Arden High School

Do You Remember That Person?

Do you remember that person?
The one they would bully and hate?
She was always in a fight,
As if it was her fate.

Do you remember that person?
The one they'd occasionally like?
And if she tried to join in,
They'd tell her to take a hike.

Do you remember that person?
From bullying she is free,
For now she is grown-up
And that person was me.

Claire Hollands (11)
Henley-in-Arden High School

Uncle

He came to my room again last night,
The house was still and there was nobody in sight,
My mum was out and my dad was away,
So my uncle felt that it was time for him to play.

I started to scream but he held my mouth
And suddenly there was silence throughout the whole of the house,
He started to touch with his own bare hands,
I felt the blood drain from me like an hourglass with sand.

The back door clicked and my mum came in
And my uncle leapt from me like he had trod on a pin,
He ran down the stairs as quiet as a cat
And started to talk to my mum about her lovely feathered hat.

The next week my dad came home from his trip
And I told him about Uncle and his nasty little tricks,
My dad phoned the police and they took him away
And now he will be in prison for the rest of his days.

Cameron Rudge (14)
Henley-in-Arden High School

The Breeze Of Summertime

As I walk the streets of England,
I feel the breeze of summertime,
I watch the trees blossoming and see their beautiful colours.

I feel the breeze of summertime,
I run my fingers across the bright red berries,
Pop one into my mouth and savour its taste.

I feel the breeze of summertime,
Shading my eyes with my hand,
I look up at the bright blue sky
And *enjoy* the breeze of summertime.

Marla Jackson (11)
Henley-in-Arden High School

Wars

Bombs exploding, destroying everything,
People darting left and right,
Houses crumbling every second,
Fire crackling, burning, scattering,
Children screaming, running for safety.

Death zone upon us,
Towns scorched, everything burned,
People petrified, shaking, crying,
Bodies buried, dirty, still,
Families broken, torn in half.

People trying to pick up the pieces,
Loved ones lost, trying to move on,
Children silent, missing lost ones,
Houses being built from demolished ruins,
Communities helping sufferers to forget.

Ellie Norton (11)
Henley-in-Arden High School

My Last Fight

My face is swollen and it hurts so much,
My sight is blurry, he looks like a smudge,
Cheers and screams, the crowd is shouting,
I hit the canvas, the ref starts counting,
The pressure is rising, my fear is high,
I can't get up and I'm thinking *why*?
Staring at the roof, the lights blind my eyes,
I'm still on the floor, much to my surprise,
The ref reaches eight, I fear the fight is up,
Coming closer to the end, I'm out of luck,
The bells sounds as the ref reaches ten,
Once the World Champion, never again.

Callum Edwards (13)
Henley-in-Arden High School

My Wish

I can move around, talk and touch,
One thing's missing in my life,
I wish my dreams could all come true,
I want to be just like you,
I need help,
Can't anybody see?
Everyone mostly,
Apart from me.
I want to see just one more time,
It all happened when I was nine,
All I remember is being hit,
After that it was the end of it,
It was coming for me, all alone,
Just as I was heading home,
Here I am after twenty years
And all I can do is wait,
Wait for the day I once began,
Back in the sky with my brand new plan.

Sophie Newey (13)
Henley-in-Arden High School

Friendship

My friends are always there for me,
They lift me up when I am down,
They help me out when I'm in need,
It's the bestest friendship you could ever lead.

We do everything together,
We go shopping,
We go hopping,
We go bowling,
We go strolling.

I have the bestest friends in the world!

Ellie Mobley (13)
Henley-in-Arden High School

Why?

Why are we here?
Is the end near
Or is it all a con?
Maybe everything is already planned,
By beings from another land,
Made up from a tube of DNA,
Who can really say?
Could this be our final day?
Form a space clan,
God was a spaceman,
Stumbled upon Earth,
Turned it into our tugs,
Took a human wife,
To make an outlook for all life,
One day, they may return,
But why?

Luke Mander (14)
Henley-in-Arden High School

Friends

It's funny how it changes,
Who your friends are,
One day they are your best friend
And the next they aren't.
They just go off with another crowd,
Walk away,
'Fine, walk away!' I say,
But really I still want you to be my friend.

I walk past you,
You don't notice me,
I look at you,
You don't look at me,
I like you,
You don't like me.

Faith Earle (13)
Henley-in-Arden High School

Baby Boy

The news breaks,
Mum's having a baby,
Is it a girl,
Or a boy maybe?

Here he is,
A beautiful boy,
Everyone jumps
And shouts for joy.

Then he goes home,
Wearing blue and white,
Staring at everything,
He can see in sight.

Cot and a playpen,
Rocking chair and more,
Everyone will love him,
I'm quite sure.

So Mummy and Daddy,
Have time to enjoy,
Their fun and love,
With this little boy.

Ellie Sams (11)
Henley-in-Arden High School

My Best Friend

Me and my best friend,
We go everywhere together,
We swim and we skate,
We shop and we talk,
She's there for me and I'm there for her,
When she laughs, I laugh,
When she cries, I cry,
I don't know what I'd do without her,
My best friend!

Katie Lukeman (13)
Henley-in-Arden High School

The Creek

Down in the creek live toads, lizards and minnows,
The little bridge going over the creek,
Little kids with canes and lines come down here to catch the fish,
The woods behind full of creatures,
Foxes, wolves and owls,
The dreaded sparrowhawk,
Enemy of mice, rats and small birds,
The creek is the waterhole,
For almost all of these creatures,
The creek, the creek where the midnight moon will sleep.

Liam Winsper (13)
Henley-in-Arden High School

The Meaning Of Life

Why have we been placed on this Earth?
What is the purpose of us being alive?
Are we being watched by other things alive?
What are we looking for or have we already found it?
Many people look to religion but are they true or fake?
Maybe the meaning of life is what you want it to be,
If it is getting rich or being free,
But in my opinion the real meaning of life is to live it!

Jordan Smith (13)
Henley-in-Arden High School

The Meaning Of Life

Do you ever think there is something out there?
Do you ever wonder what you could do?
Sometimes I wish I knew,
People ask God questions but sometimes you think,
Who are they talking to?
The Bible tells us things we do not know,
But now people think they know everything.

Jack Dargov (14)
Henley-in-Arden High School

A Possum's Life

Possums are great,
Possums are small,
But when they stand up they are very tall,
They are fluffy and cream with a hint of brown,
They can also be annoying and very loud,
They look like rats,
They live up a tree,
They have to go out and catch their own tea,
They eat fruit and berries,
They live in a hole,
But at the zoo they eat from a bowl,
That is what a possum is like,
One more thing,
They are impolite!

Sam Thirlaway (13)
Henley-in-Arden High School

Horses

Horses, they could jump the moon,
I recommend riding them,
I'd do it very soon,
You can walk, canter and trot,
A bridle and saddle is all you've got,
You put your foot in the stirrup,
You hold on to the reins,
You hold them too loose and they'll be a pain,
You groom them with a brush,
You'd better do it properly, you don't need to rush,
If I see you riding you'll be like *hooray,*
I bet you'll be really happy,
Until you fall off one day.

Alice Longe (11)
Henley-in-Arden High School

Spiders

Scary, hairy little things,
Lucky they don't have wings,
They can run like a train,
But they don't like the rain.

Big ones, small ones, all ones,
Don't like songs!
People say they bite,
They come out at night.

Poisonous or not,
There are quite a lot,
Insects are their meal,
You can find them west to east.

Web spinning,
Never swimming,
We're scared of them,
Or are they scared of us?

Sophie Castle (11)
Henley-in-Arden High School

Cancer

Cancer is spread all over the world,
People suffer from it all the time,
Don't put yourself down,
You'll pull through,
Like many who have and will,
This part of life is just a mountain,
Be strong and climb this mountain,
Do not give up and fall down,
You have the rest of your life to fulfil.

Adam Carless (13)
Henley-in-Arden High School

The Monster In The Nook

I was lying in my bed,
With my fists held tight,
My sheet was over my head,
For it seemed the darkest night!

I knew that it was in there,
I had heard it make a sound,
Look at it - I didn't dare,
For I knew what I had found!

The monster in the nook,
Was waiting there for me,
I really couldn't bear to look,
Afraid what I might see!

I felt it touch my head,
I felt it shake my knee,
A voice close by me said,
'It's Dad, do you want your tea?'

Grace Sharp (11)
Henley-in-Arden High School

Who Is It?

He lies under your bed,
He lurks in the darkness,
He watches you day and night,
Staring with his beady eye,
He eats spiders and other living things,
Until a foot out of bed,
It hits the floor, he sees his prey,
He eats you instead,
Who is it? No one knows,
He lives where no one goes.

Eleanor Gorton (11)
Henley-in-Arden High School

The Monster Under My Bed

A monster lives under my bed,
He has big wide eyes,
Which glare at you in the darkness,
His sharp, needle-like teeth stick out,
Trying to reach out and snap at you.

His ears twitch,
Listening for every sound,
His black, rough skin,
Brushes against the bed,
Sometimes you can almost feel it,
That is the monster who lives under my bed!

Eleanor Parsons (11)
Henley-in-Arden High School

War

I'm lying awake in my bed,
Hearing all sorts of things in my head.

Houses collapsing, lots of rubble,
Surely the sirens must mean trouble.

Reading a book, singing songs,
Nothing will stop me from hearing those bombs.

It gets worse when the floor starts to shake,
A plane has just crashed - what noise it does make.

The bombs are all finished except for just one,
It landed on me, so now I'm all gone.

Alice McAlear (11)
Henley-in-Arden High School

The Diablos

The Diablos is a terrible beast,
It burrows through the ground,
However, to get it angry use a rather loud sound,
It has horns as sharp as daggers,
Thick as a human head,
But if it changes you'd be better off dead,
It has a spiky tail club and it will hit you,
The wound would need more than just a rub,
It has scales like a wizard,
But on its back there are two shells,
Towns were unprepared for this beast,
So all they did was ring a bell before it unleashed hell.

William Riley (11)
Henley-in-Arden High School

A Beaten Child

I'm sat in this dark room,
He's about to hit me with this broom,
I'd try to run away but he'll hit me harder,
He's not a very good father,
He took me in as his own,
But this is Hell, not home,
Mum's away at work, away from him,
But I'm still here and life's so grim,
I wish I could escape from this prison I'm in,
I wish I could run away from this dark room,
But he'll find me and kill me with his broom.

Kaylee Gill (13)
Henley-in-Arden High School

Lying Awake

Lying here, now awake,
Once again the explosion too loud,
Like it has been since it started,
What have I done wrong?
Do I deserve this?

My nightmares screaming,
Shouting at me,
People suffering all around,
The gun's bullet screeching in my ears,
Bombs falling everywhere.

People along with them,
Homes and cities being cruelly destroyed,
So they run and try to get free,
Soldiers not caring just capturing,
Family and friends probably never to be seen again.

So I lie waiting,
Waiting for my nightmares,
Waiting for the shouting,
Waiting for the screaming,
Waiting for the bombs.

I'll close my eyes,
I'll try to block it out,
Until once again,
It will happen and it will feel,
Like it will never stop.

Sophia Locke (11)
Henley-in-Arden High School

Climate Change

In the Arctic soon it will just be a sea,
A warm one at that,
Over here in the UK
It will soon be hotter than Australia,
So we'll all have to scrap
Our woolly hats!

Soon there won't be any trees
Because they're all being bulldozed for land,
The rainforest is also being killed
Because of the lack of rain!

We will soon be walking
Around like chimney sweeps
Because of the clouds of smoke,
We shall all be coughing
Like we've smoked sixty a
Day all our lives.

Everywhere we go all we will see
Is power stations giving off tons of smoke,
What I would like to know is where the wind farms are!

Katie Lester (11)
Henley-in-Arden High School

England Delights

London has the spinning Eye,
Cornwall has the pasty and pie,
Manchester has the X-Factor winner,
Birmingham's Bull Ring serves your dinner.

Warwick's castle, a popular place,
Nottingham's soft silky lace,
Newcastle's beer is quite fine,
York is the place to go and dine.

Charlotte Thomas (12)
Henley-in-Arden High School

Untitled

Leaves rustling,
Hedgehogs snuffling,
Stumbling across the lawn.

Diggers accelerating,
Deafening digging,
Ruining their habitat.

Sheep bleating,
Lambs skipping across the field,
Tawny owls hooting,
Mice squeaking, as a predator swoops down.

The roar of an aeroplane,
Thunderous roaring,
Ruining their environment.

Deer sauntering,
Rabbits scurrying away from the road,
Cuckoos echoing across the valley.

Fires sizzling,
Burning, blazing,
Ruining their environment.

Luke Ogden (11)
Henley-in-Arden High School

Football

Football is a brilliant game,
That anyone can play,
With skills, and style, you will always aim,
To win the game some day.

The ball moves past fast and smooth,
Into the net it lands,
Then you hear the uproar of everyone
And a bunch of clapping hands.

Lewis Hartle (12)
Henley-in-Arden High School

No Contact!

No contact they say for this game with a ball,
Played by fit women and girls who are tall,
Line up for the pass and aim for the net,
It's played in all weather, both dry and wet,
The aim of the game is to try and score,
The winning team is the one who gets more,
Each position has a job to do,
You can defend or attack, there's a centre too!
Listen for the whistle and the umpire's call,
Don't move your feet, it's the footwork rule,
Dodge and sprint and keep your space,
It's against the clock so keep up the pace,
Hustle and bustle, movement and speed,
Netball's the game, *no contact indeed!*

Lucy McDermott (11)
Henley-in-Arden High School

Troubles In The World

War, war all around,
Bombs give off the loudest sound,
People killing, people dying,
All are hurt, you hear them sighing,
Global warming isn't stopping,
The tree cutters don't stop chopping,
But there's still hope in the world,
Things can change with just one word,
Stop polluting as best you can,
Stopping these is the greatest plan!

Charlie Meadows (11)
Henley-in-Arden High School

Torturing Teachers

Mr Wilson, king of sarcasm,
Forgetting science and loving games,
Staring over us with his towering height.

Mr Davis, computer freak,
Sorting out vile viruses on the computer,
Shouting aloud, 'Saint David's are the best.'

Miss Turner, stunning pianist,
Yet the best singer in the whole school,
Helping us write magnificent stories.

Mr Carnell, boss of the school,
We do not know what we would do without him,
As he is the kindest and most friendly headmaster of all.

Teachers are terrible, like fingernails grinding down a blackboard,
Teachers are terrific, like mountains of chocolate,
But they will always be forever in your *memory*.

Paramvir Dhanda (11)
St Martin's School, Solihull

King Of The Wood

The king of the wood casts his piercing eyes
Down upon the gloomy forest,
He sits on the branch of a winding tree,
The gleaming moon beams dimly,
Murky clouds drift around,
Trees groan and whisper and leaves glide slowly to the floor,
Another owl sweeps down catching its prey,
Its talons grip the tiny mouse that it has caught,
Groping around in the dark, a squirrel pops his head out of a tree,
The wood is silent,
All that can be heard is the wind barging its way through the trees
And the occasional hoot from the owls.

Emily Blake (12)
St Martin's School, Solihull

Who Am I?

It is just me on my own,
Me all alone,
My own thoughts,
My own feelings.

Something to think about,
Learn about, talk about,
Nobody else is like me,
Nobody shares the same thoughts,
Am I alone
Or is there someone like me?

My spirit is young and free,
So many things to see -
My ideas are unique
And so
Am
I.

Anna O'Connell (12)
St Martin's School, Solihull

Into Her Head

People think she just sits and stares,
Staring out into space,
But in this head there is much more than that,
What you see is not just a girl,
Sitting, staring out into space.
Oh no!
What you see is a mind full of thoughts,
An imagination so full it could burst!
But what goes on in this head?
Nobody knows except that girl that just sits there and stares.

Charlotte Beaty (11)
St Martin's School, Solihull

Old Grace's Racing Days

Pressurising voices,
'Come on Shooting Star.'
Chasing the same old rabbit,
Across the finishing line,
Scolding voices directed at her,
Every other dog receives a medal,
Grace is dragged away in disgrace.

Her legs ache so much,
Her arthritis is creeping in,
Thrown in a van, darkness sets in,
The lock clicks and Grace drifts into sleep,
The screech of tyres and a jangle of keys,
She is hauled out of the van.

She is dumped by the highway,
Cars racing past like the track,
Only a few people glance,
Eventually one car stops.

A kind, gentle voice speaks softly and slowly,
A warm blanket is spread over her
As she is placed in a car,
Now in a warm comforting home,
Poor old Grace, she used to race,
She now lives her life at her own pace.

Georgina Freeman (12)
St Martin's School, Solihull

Once Upon A Dream

When I am lying in my bed,
The hectic world around me seems to halt,
All my thoughts dash through my head,
Then I steadily drift to sleep,
A dim black light gradually gets lighter,
The light suddenly turns into a spectacular place.

Mountains with glistening snow surround me,
An Arctic wolf's eyes glaze,
I walk along and the snow crunches,
The wind howls and a cold breeze brushes past,
As I continue walking I hit thick fog,
I can barely see anything,
Then I slip and fall down the mountain,
All I can see is a black pit,
It is waiting to gulp me up.

I wake up in a shock as my window slams,
With the feeling that my stomach is in my throat,
I go to close my window,
The dream seemed to take forever
But only seconds had passed,
Then I drifted to sleep again,
Waiting to have another adventure.

Lucy Phillpots (12)
St Martin's School, Solihull

The Sea

An open clear page, ready for exploration,
Things to discover,
Things to see.

Sea creatures gathering around me,
Their beautiful skin,
Their elegance,
I am swallowed in.

The children running in,
Catching the cold waves,
Seagulls and herons,
The fish of the day!

The divine sunset,
All colours shining through,
You try to catch it,
But soon it is gone.

Emily Sumnall (12)
St Martin's School, Solihull

Conkers

Autumn time is here again,
The horse chestnut tree tells me so,
Every year I can't wait,
To knock some down with my mate.

Using sticks, balancing on shoulders,
It's not always easy to get them down,
The spiky shell sometimes pricks me,
As it's not ready to leave the tree.

I look inside, it's not always ripe,
As it's not brown but white,
Conkers one, two, or three,
Inside a shell from the horse chestnut tree.

Amy Charlotte Parsons (11)
St Martin's School, Solihull

Today

Today is unique,
Yesterday is long gone
And tomorrow shall be different.

Things that happen today,
Things I think,
People I see and hear,
Are the future memories of tomorrow.

No one's day is the same,
Everyone sees and thinks different things,
Yet we are all living the same day.

Our memories are slipping through our fingers,
We are like a memory stick,
The older we get the less memory we store,
But some things we cannot forget.

I was born on a unique day,
A unique person, to a unique family,
At a unique time, only mine.

The past hour is now a memory,
Gone,
It shall not return,
Never to be witnessed again.

Like a magic book,
Which you can only turn the pages forward,
To move on in the story.

Going back is not a possibility,
It is now and for evermore just memories,
We cannot change the past,
However much we may want to.

Today is unique,
Yesterday is long gone
And tomorrow shall be different.

Stephanie Hines (12)
St Martin's School, Solihull

Away With Words

As I sat down in the classroom,
Sat and chewed my pen,
We had to write a poem,
But the teacher was groaning and moaning,
No you can't write a poem about a hen!

I started out of the window,
It looked like I was watching the netball,
I wasn't,
I was away with the words again.

People said I was away with the fairies,
Whey can't they understand,
I'm not out with the fairies,
I'm away with the words instead!

The words were so amazing,
They jumbled in my head,
A, B, C, D comma (,) E, F, G full stop (.)
I always got an F,
I just couldn't understand,
I wasn't away with the fairies,
I was on holiday with the words instead.

When I'm thinking of the answers,
The words just come and invade my head,
Why can't they understand me?
I'm not dancing with the fairies,
I'm playing with the words instead!

Whatever I stop to look at
And read those marvellous words,
When I've had enough they tell me,
'Back to reality,'
The fairies have gone to bed,
They just don't understand,
I'm away with the words instead.

Those silly fairies don't exist,
They never enter my head,
Why can't they understand me?
It's not fairies in my head but words instead.

My head is my head,
But no one understands, they can't see inside it,
It isn't theirs to keep,
They just can't see inside it, if only,
If they could,
They would see the fairies don't exist,
But they might just spot a word or two instead!

Emily Bridges (11)
St Martin's School, Solihull

The White Wolf

Her deep brown pads indent the snow,
Unnoticed, she wanders by,
Sleek as a fox,
Swift as a bird,
Her prize, she holds up high.

Her snow-white coat stands out so strong,
Though no one sees her pass,
Careful as a newborn pup,
Silent as a hunting lynx,
She runs across the grass.

So, no one sees the white wolf fall,
As crimson drowns her pelt,
Fast as light,
Sharp as knife,
The hunter claims his kill.

No longer can she roam this earth,
Her spirit always here,
Dead and gone,
Though through it all,
Her spirit lingers on.

Lucy Parkes (12)
St Martin's School, Solihull

The Colours Of The Rainbow!

Red is the colour of the rainbow,
Rich, warm, fiery red,
It comforts you when said.

Orange is the colour of the rainbow,
Orange is bright and fun,
It puts a smile on your face when everything is done.

Yellow is the colour of the rainbow,
Sunny yellow reminds us of the summer sun,
It keeps us running throughout the day.

Green is the colour of the rainbow,
Fresh, wet, grassy green,
It reminds us of nature.

Blue is the colour of the rainbow,
Ice-cold blue,
It cools us down on a hot sticky day.

Indigo is the colour of the rainbow,
Dark, smooth indigo,
It relaxes us at the end of the day.

Violet is the colour of the rainbow,
Sleepy violet,
It puts you to bed when late at night.

The rainbow,
It keeps us happy throughout our lives.

Emma Voogd (11)
St Martin's School, Solihull

Midsummer Night Dream

As I lie in my dream boat
And I begin to clear my head,
I feel like I am sinking,
Right through my cosy bed,
I then just start dreaming,
As I drift off,
I sail on a turquoise ocean,
With beautiful lavender smells,
I then feel as if I've got wings
And I'm floating in mid-air,
High above the clouds,
I circle the top of dreamland,
I feel the freedom that I have,
Suddenly . . . I'm falling, falling,
Falling to my bed,
I then arrive with a bump,
Alarm clock beeping, Mum and Dad yelling,
'Wake up you sleepyhead!'

Emma Wilson (13)
St Martin's School, Solihull

My Hand

My writing bump is on my right hand
And it likes to hold a wand,
My hand is busy as a bee,
Because it always wants to touch and see,
I have a brown beauty spot on my palm,
At rest, my hand is still and calm,
My hiding hands are flexible,
That is why they are not visible,
My hand lines tell about my life,
My fingerprints are,
Printing the pages,
My hand is my signature.

Julia Cornet (11)
St Martin's School, Solihull

Our World

Our world is ever changing,
Shrinking and growing,
The plates are moving, the sea is deepening
And volcanoes erupting, tornadoes roaring.

The sea eroding the cliffs,
While ice caps are melting,
Sea levels rising bringing
Huge chances of tsunamis.

Volcanoes erupt, turning cities to ash,
But some are sleeping,
Building up for a huge explosion,
Just waiting for boiling lava to explode.

The jungles and rainforests cut down unjustly,
As Australia's forests burst into flame,
Under the scorching heat,
Of the frazzling sun.

Tornadoes raging through the world,
Like a tiger ripping and shredding up cities,
Whipped up by the wind,
Destroying civilisation as they go.

Our world is ever changing,
Shrinking and growing,
Changing as we speak,
We are the only ones who can save *our* world.

Rhiannon Thomas (12)
St Martin's School, Solihull

Hopes And Dreams

As night-time approaches,
I get tucked up in bed,
Lying there comfy,
Mulling over all that's been said.
Has it been a good day
Or has it been bad?
Will I wake up in the morning,
Feeling happy or sad?

Soon my eyelids get heavy
And I fall off to sleep,
Visions appear,
Both vivid and deep,
Magical lands fill my mind,
Adventures and mystery take up their part,
People, places, unreal and true,
All these things taking over my heart.

A land of my own,
All of mine to explore,
Being crowned as the queen
Or maybe serving the poor,
Being an actor or a singer,
Everyone at my feet,
Places to go
And people to meet.

These dreams so wonderful,
Do not always appear,
Nightmares abound
Like galloping deer,
Being kidnapped and orphaned,
My greatest of fears,
Suddenly I wake up,
My eyes filled with tears.

Hannah Jesani (12)
St Martin's School, Solihull

Tenants Of The Earth

Remember the world when there were no humans,
No corruption, freedom,
Mossy hills looking over the world with protecting eyes,
Magnificent oak trees,
Guardians of the forest, standing tall and proud,
Animals free, roaming the countryside,
But this was soon to change.

Humans were born, technology evolved,
Mossy hills made into mere slaves,
Oak trees cut down to stumps,
Dirty tarmac destroying the environment's home,
Wars in every country.

Hunters chasing after innocent animals,
No compassion, no soul
And with a bang most animals are dead.

At a rapid pace the world is being destroyed,
However, it is not ours to destroy,
Nature is the landlord and we are the tenants.

Jessica Whitehouse-Lowe (12)
St Martin's School, Solihull

I Am Myself

My hand has touched so many possessions,
Some bright and wonderful!
It has brought so many memories,
Some fabulous and some not,
My hand has touched my mum and dad's hands,
My brother's too,
It has touched my nan and grandad,
Family, friends and the rest of the crew,
My hand has touched animals of all different types,
My hand helps me play tennis on a Sunday,
It helps me hold a hockey stick and other great things too!

Harriet Levett-Dunn (11)
St Martin's School, Solihull

Disasters Of The World

Tornadoes spin round the world,
Ripping it up like paper,
So many lives and houses lost,
Nothing could ever repay the cost,
Of the natural disasters of the world.

Oceans roar raging with anger,
As tidal waves crash onto beaches,
Sucking out life like leeches,
What is going on with the world?

Volcanoes exploding all over the world,
As lava and ash come spilling out,
Like an overflowing teacup,
The world is eroding gradually each day,
Soon we shall be no more.

The Earth shakes vigorously,
As people's screams make windows shatter,
Many humans fear the end,
But the terror is just beginning.

Sarah Tibbetts (12)
St Martin's School, Solihull

My Hand

This is the hand my mother held,
When I first crossed the road,
This hand is the hand that held the pen
That I wrote with when I was shown,
This hand is my hand,
Unique and like no other,
With shapes and bumps and writing lumps,
Bones and skin and lines so thin,
This hand will lead and guide me through all my living days,
Where I can wave and clap and shake hands in friendship
And close together with my other when I pray.

Naomi Hemming (11)
St Martin's School, Solihull

Cherish Your Visions And Dreams

Always be yourself,
You are very special and unique,
There is no one on Earth like you,
Cherish your visions and dreams.

Never give up your hopes,
Let nobody steal them from you,
Be determined, keep heading for your goal,
Cherish your visions and dreams.

Don't let people change you,
Stand apart from the crowd,
Be as focused as a leopard stalking its prey,
Cherish your visions and dreams.

Stand up, believe in yourself,
You can change the world,
Aim high like a shooting arrow,
Cherish your visions and dreams.

Eleanor Bhasin (12)
St Martin's School, Solihull

I Am Myself

I am my hands and my hands are me,
My hands are like an actress,
They play many parts,
The best part is belonging to me.

I have happy hands, helpful hands and hockey hands,
My hands are busy hands but they are still soft and slender,
Just as a potter moulds his clay,
All that I do with my hands moulds me,
This is the hand that touched the starfish in the Caribbean Sea,
This is the hand which has a writing lump,
This is the hand that an athletics spike went through,
These are the hands that you can see,
These are the hands that belong to me.

Anna Trenchard (11)
St Martin's School, Solihull

The Sea

The sea is a blanket of everlasting peace,
Clear and blue, calm and pure,
Never fading, a gentle force,
Like shimmering crystals, the ripples grow,
As the water warms from the frying sun,
The water is as still as a sheet of glass,
Yet as deep as Everest is high.

The sea is ever changing, colours, emotions and tide.

The sea is a pride of lions full of hate and death,
Murky and grey, rough and stirred,
Brutal and scary, a violent force,
A giant mouth spreading across a million miles of black doom,
The submerged figures,
In the dark, gloomy water dance and play,
While the eerie surroundings suck in the fearless swimmers.

The sea is ever changing, colours, emotions and tide.

Brooke Jones (12)
St Martin's School, Solihull

My Hand

My hand,
Unique, my own, my special effect,
Long thin fingers ending in bitten fingernails,
Square and blunt,
I turn over my hand and find creases
And bumps like whiplash upon my hand.

My hand, my knuckles,
My baby knuckles, all scarred, battered and scraped,
Blue veins sticking out of my hand like blue on white.

I am myself, like my hand,
I am unique; I am myself,
My hand that no one else will ever own!

Natasha Woodley (11)
St Martin's School, Solihull

The Sea Washing Away With Words

The sea washing away with words,
The spray and the waves,
The whirls of the ebbing tides,
Dashing against the seashore.

The sea washing away with words,
The tastes and the smells,
The aroma of the freshly caught fish
And the tang of seaweed on the seashore.

The sea washing away with words,
The colours and the shades,
The tinge of blue and green
And the sparkle and shimmer of the sunlit sea.

The sea washing away with words,
The noises and relentless commotion,
The squawking of the gulls
And the smacking of the waves against the bobbing boats.

The sea washing away with words,
Pulling in and out
And taking everything with it,
Including my own words, feelings and dreams.

Francesca Ward (11)
St Martin's School, Solihull

Music

I put on my radio,
Waiting for the sound,
I press the play button,
On this old CD I've found.

The music comes over me,
I'm no longer stressed, I'm free!
Track two is ending now,
Coming onto track three.

Rock, hip hop, dance,
So many types of music!
The beat is getting louder,
I no longer can hear the acoustic.

It's getting really dark,
But I'm not tired one bit!
I am getting cold though,
So it is the fire I lit.

The sound of Beethoven's First Symphony,
Makes me tired alright!
I fling myself on the sofa
And say to myself, 'Goodnight!'

Marianna Avgousti (11)
St Martin's School, Solihull

School

School, the building of knowledge for all,
The subjects haunt the halls and classes,
People, places and familiar faces,
As the secrets climb the walls and doors.

Corridors, the tunnels of travel and transport,
The bell rings as the noises rise,
The silence has vanished among the walls,
The bell rings, once more the silence crawls out.

The playground, the ground of freedom and fun,
As the students emerge, the ground is in use,
They play around and jump and skip,
Along the lush, green grass.

Home time, the time for home and rest,
The car park is like a cattle herd, it is always full and noisy,
Your mother appears in a mechanic coloured monster,
Which is raring to take you home.

Samantha Penney (11)
St Martin's School, Solihull

My Mind

My mind opens like a flower bursting into the start of a new day,
In there is chocolate, that melting sensation sweet but bitter,
A swan gliding through the cold icy lake on a winter's morning.

And there is a sea gushing up onto the shore of the sandbanks,
The boats bobbing on the horizon, all in time with the current.

There is a penguin,
That flies in the clear blue sky.

There is a secret diary,
There I sit, fingering the pages of my life, my dreams.

I know that I can't be cut or shaped into someone else.

I am the only me in the whole of this world, I am unique.

Nicole Inman (11)
St Martin's School, Solihull

What I Love

I love to eat ice cream,
It tastes so cool and fresh,
My tongue has a party when I eat it,
It is like a tasty polar bear diving into my mouth.

I love to eat chocolate,
It tastes so warm and milky,
The luxurious taste slowly melts through my lips,
It's like a sunshine, lovely, beautiful, shining in my mouth.

I love to play netball,
It is a fun, active sport to play,
It keeps me busy, fit and lively,
It reminds me of a fast cheetah when I dodge into a space.

I love to cycle on my bike,
My legs go round and round like the London Eye,
I get dizzy if I stare at them for just a second,
My brakes screech like a crying baby when I stop in alarm.

I love to talk to my friends,
They are so chatty and friendly,
My friends are always there for me when I am upset,
They treat me as if I am a pop star singing to a big crowd.

I love to talk to my family,
They are so kind and caring,
My family never tease me, be nasty or bully me,
They treat me as if I am a queen ruling a country proudly.

Hopefully, no one will ever take the things I love away from me,
Especially my friends and family.

Molly Eales (11)
St Martin's School, Solihull

Fireworks

Bang!
The fireworks begin,
Different colours glide through the sky,
Pink starbursts, yellow explosions,
Squealing rockets and a flash of light.

Fizz!
People holding sparklers,
The sparklers twinkle as you look at them,
Golden stars in the sky,
That is what they are.

Hiss!
Whirling fireworks have begun,
They whirl and leave a long silver line across the sky,
It is like a snail's trail,
On the ground outside.

Flash!
A huge umbrella opens,
It shimmers so much it feels like you are blinking all the time,
It flies down towards me,
It never reaches me.

Amy Bullard (11)
St Martin's School, Solihull

Winter

The snow prickled
And popped at my feet
And a shiver tickled,
On my soft cold skin.

The little snowman in his blue scarf and gloves.

My eye caught sight of
The bare trees
And the silhouette on the ground.

The leaves on the ground,
The crunch when you step on them.

The sound you hear if you listen carefully,
The whistle of the leaves blowing into the sky.

The dull sky,
As black as ever,
Like a scary, moody face staring at you,
Staring at you.

The winter weather.

Charlotte Taylor (11)
St Martin's School, Solihull

The Seaside

Today I'm at the seaside,
I can see lots of things here,
Like people building sandcastles and playing in the sea,
Some people are even on stripy red deckchairs
And having a rest, looking at the vast ocean blue.

At the seaside I can hear lots of little voices,
Shouting and screaming,
I can also hear seagull's chirping,
Pinching all of the fish and chips,
Oh, I mustn't forget the turquoise sea,
It's making a lovely swishing sound, it's beautiful.

Mmm, I can smell scrumptious fish and chips,
I think it's about time I had some of those,
They smell delicious,
What else can I smell?
I can smell the sand with all the shells on it and seaweed,
The whole smell of the seaside is so nice.

At the seaside I can touch the pale yellow sand
And touch the water letting it trickle through my hands,
It's cold! I also had a pinch on the finger by a crab,
Ouch!
There are also lots of little rock pools,
So I can feel the slippery, wet, slimy seaweed,
Ewe horrible!

The feeling of going to the seaside is great,
Although it's such a great feeling when you have to come home,
But still, it's always great being able to spend a day at the seaside
And have lots of fun and memories to take home with you.

Esther Byrne (11)
St Martin's School, Solihull

A Ferrari

A Ferrari drives nearly as fast as a cheetah,
It's shiny like a crystal,
It's smoother than cats' fur.

The Ferrari sounds like a lion roaring for food,
It has the latest sports kit of the year,
It is the most gleaming, beautiful red there is.

The interior is fiery orange with black suede in-between,
The wheel is red and black just like the door panel,
The sound system is the latest technology with
TV, satellite navigation and an MP3 player.

On the outside are side skirts and dark blue flames,
There are neon lights underneath,
This Ferrari is the *best Ferrari in the world!*

Karlissa Khan (11)
St Martin's School, Solihull

There I Am, Myself

My hand has pummelled a decaying wall,
This hand has shot the scoring netball.

A blemish, a scar extended across my hand,
Wrapped around tight like a rubber band.

Some people's hands help them to run at a faster pace,
But my hand works hard and wipes a teary face.

My hand has happily tickled a purring cheetah,
My hand has gone through pain.

This hand is unique,
No one else's is the same.

Evie Matthews-Jolly (11)
St Martin's School, Solihull

My Hands Are Mine

My hands are bumpy,
My nails are short.

I have white scuffs,
I have hand wrinkles.

My knuckles are smooth,
I have a hill like writing bump,
My hands are rough.

I have three lifelines and
One of them is curved.

I have scars on my hand
That has touched so many animals and
It feels like my hand has touched the world.

My hands have waved hello,
My hands have waved goodbye.

This is the hand that writes emails and taps,
Scratches and strokes.

My hand has been to so many places,
My hand has stroked so many animals,
My hand is the hand that writes this poem.

My hand has a life,
Of its own.

Princess Adenuga (11)
St Martin's School, Solihull

Things I Love

The things I love
Come in small packages,
In parcels, in presents,
In bags.

The things I love
Dancing,
I love dancing in
Competitions.

The things I love
My family,
I love the way
They laugh at me.

The things I love
Water skiing,
I love the way,
My skis float on the water.

The things I love
Swimming,
I love the way,
You glide through the water.

These are all the
Things I love.

Anabel Badham (11)
St Martin's School, Solihull

God's Creation

My hand is a sculpture,
Fingers modelled with clay,
Nails painted with acrylic paints,
Veins carved from the finest pine,
Knuckles controlled by electric power,
Each one of our hands is different,
A different sculpture, a different model,
We use these fascinating machines,
To control a lot of our life,
What we do and how we do it,
This fine piece of art was modelled by God,
The technology we use to touch and to feel,
Just imagine,
How many sculptures He modelled,
How many abilities He created,
How many hands He made
And yet each one is different.

Abigail Rogers (11)
St Martin's School, Solihull

My Hands Like No Others

My hand is special,
Different to anyone else's,
Medium-sized,
Four fingers and a thumb,
White marks on the nails
And scars on my palm.

Has softly touched a foal,
An elephant too,
Leathery skin and grey like a cloud,
My fingerprint is individual,
Going up like a mountain
And across like the sea,
My hand belongs to me.

Sophie Yelloly (11)
St Martin's School, Solihull

Inside My Head!

My head is filled with countless thoughts always.

Wishing to be a professional cheerleader,
The endless homework piles up
And counting down to the weekend.

The thoughts of going outside to the bitter cold winter,
To go to school in the morning,
Talking for ages to my friends on the phone.

Worrying about getting good marks at school,
Chocolate, chocolate, I want more of it all the time.

My mum nagging me to clean my room and keep it that way,
My dad telling me not to put off my homework any longer,
How sad it is to watch people and animals die in pain.

These thoughts fill my head right now,
But all of my thoughts are never-ending.

Sydney Voeffray (11)
St Martin's School, Solihull

My Hand

My hands are like my mum's,
My fingers bend the same way.

Long, strong nails I paint in reds and pinks,
Depending on what mood I am in,
My nails are shaped, square and round,
The rings I wear which sparkle and shine.

Lines carved into my palms,
Ridges and veins I see so clear,
My thumbprint, my identity is mine alone,
The whorls on my thumb go round and round.

Emotions, I have felt over the years,
The bumps, the bruises, the memories I will always hold.

Simran Sunner (11)
St Martin's School, Solihull

These Hands Have A Soft Touch

These hands have a soft touch,
Gentle, caressing like silk on smooth skin,
Fingers so long with nails shaped and pink
They are always so active on keyboards, zips and pens,
One hand has a watch and perfect diamond ring,
The other a bracelet and bumps,
But they never lose their soft touch.

These hands have a soft touch,
Holding hands as we cross the road,
For comfort when I need it the most,
Lifelines telling me what I shall be,
Who I shall marry and how many kids there will be,
These hands hold my identity,
Who I am, my DNA,
Nobody can change what my hands are,
Whether they like it or not.

These hands have a soft touch,
These are the hands that have touched a house made only of shells,
These are the hands that give other people signals,
These are the hands that I will love always,
These hands have a soft touch.

Molly Norton (11)
St Martin's School, Solihull

The Lost Garden

I open the rusty gate and creep into the lost garden
Walking through the arch of sunflowers,
The rotten wooden bridge over the trickling stream,
The birds swoop from the trees and their extraordinary nests,
The diamond flowers glisten in the bright sunshine,
The bunnies, squirrels and magical creatures roam freely,
Unicorns and ponies jump around playing with ribbons
And jumping over the rainbows.

The tiny fairies and pixies leave a trail of dust and glitter,
The secret garden, my own, nobody knows,
A secret . . . a secret for life.

Delightful, cheerful, magical, merry words,
To explain what this lost garden has.

Love, love is the key to this secret garden,
If you have no love the gate will not open,
It is too strong to be defeated, however forced.

There is no wall to be climbed and no gate to be opened,
With no love.

A secret . . . a secret for life.

Georgia Tarn (12)
St Martin's School, Solihull

My Hand

My hand,
So many lines,
What do they all mean?
A few of them are scratches,
Fiery red lashes across my hand.

My hand,
It has done so many things,
It has done my homework,
It has written an exam,
It has been shopping.

My hand,
It has done 'hi-fives' to the people in the netball team,
When we score goals,
It has brushed my hair,
It has put my make-up on.

My hand,
It is my hand only,
No one can have my hand,
Everyone has their own hand,
My hand is unique, it is only mine.

Katherine Spittle (11)
St Martin's School, Solihull

I Am Myself

My hand is different,
Unique,
It has a jungle of lines and marks,
That make me individual.

My hand makes me myself,
The things that it has touched,
Like when it wiped away my tears,
When I left my primary school.

My hand has helped me do things,
To press the keys on a keyboard and type this poem,
Without it I would not be complete
And wouldn't be able to feel and touch the world.

My hand has short square nails
And a writing bump,
Bony knuckles and a long lifeline
And calved-out lines on my palms.

My hand is very different,
Unique,
It has a jungle of lines and marks,
That make me individual.

Krittika Sharma (11)
St Martin's School, Solihull

Think Of The Hands

Think of the hands that built your house,
The house you live in today,
Think of the hands that built The Opera House,
The place you visit today.

Think of the hands that built the boats,
The boats you sail today,
Think of the hands that wipe away
The tears you shed today,
We should all be grateful for such wonderful things,
Because some of us take them for granted.

My hands are two different living things,
A useful pair,
With swirls and whorls and wheels,
Of fun to help complete the list of things to do.

My hands have different DNA to all others
And write my name,
My own signature!

Nicola Skakel (11)
St Martin's School, Solihull

Me, Myself And I

Looking at my hand,
If only it could talk,
It would tell many tales of my life,
Past,
Present
And future.

My hand touched my brother when he was born,
It held my cousin's hand when he learnt to walk,
It touched The Tower of Pisa when I was only eight,
It helped keep my balance when I learnt to skate.

My little hand,
Has its own identity,
No one can have the same,
No one but me,
My hand will experience it all,
Everything that this life has to offer.

Sophie Griesbach (11)
St Martin's School, Solihull

I Am Myself

I am myself,
Different fingertips,
Left and right swerves and curves,
My hand.

My mind no one can touch,
My thoughts only I can control,
Fishes and dishes, only my wishes!
My self.

This is the hand with scars and cuts,
Bruises that have healed over time,
My hand,
All mine.

The things I've touched,
Walls, toys, the single tear down my cheek,
My hand.

My sport,
The javelin throw,
Passing on the relay baton,
Now, now, now, all of my know-how,
My hands.

When me and my hands go down to die,
The things I've touched will be there,
My hand should really take it easy,
But it can't because I'm very busy.

Abigail Watts (11)
St Martin's School, Solihull

My Hand

My hand,
Everything about it is so different,
The way I have more wrinkles on one than the other,
The way each bit of hair on my fingers is different,
My hands are very smooth
And my nail-bitten fingers that have started to grow.

Each thing on my hand is different,
Different to my friends,
Even different to my family,
My hand has so many memories,
When I burnt it on the boiling oven,
When I wiped the tears away when Olivia Thompson left,
When I fell over they would pick me back up again
And the hand that wiped away my tears from my bright red face.

My hand has done so much,
Felt so much
And even seen so much,
These are the hands that have jumped when they burn
On something hot,
They are the hands that have moved away suddenly
When something is freezing cold,
My hands have been through so much,
They have been with me everywhere I've been,
These are the hands that will stay with me forever,
Through my journey of life.

Anna Joyce (11)
St Martin's School, Solihull

Making My Mark Upon The World

My hands,
Touching, feeling,
Holding, creating,
Understanding,
Lines and creases carved with care.

Individual,
Completely different to anyone else's,
Completely my own,
Weathered and changed by experiences and emotions.

Hugs,
A crinkled sheet of paper with my signature all over it,
My signature, my hand print,
Mine alone.

This hand has welcomed,
But always waved goodbye,
It has dried tears of sadness,
But has also rejoiced,
It has been shy and timid,
But also loud and angry.

My hands have a voice of their own,
Telling thousands of stories of places they have been,
Things they have held and things they have made,
They hold many secrets,
They tell of lifestyles and changing characters.

Forever changing, forever growing,
Then joining together with one another to make a whole.

They are individual,
They are their own entity.

Sophie Tillman (11)
St Martin's School, Solihull

The Lost Garden

The arched door creaks as I push it to,
It was a garden,
A lost garden,
Like a labyrinth of lost dreams.

The malevolent ivy smothers and chokes the antiquated brick,
As it crawls up the wall's edges,
Wisps of icy breath from the trees creep over my skin,
As they silently move from side to side.

A strong sense of abandonment pervades the air,
As I meander on through the crumbled limestone paths,
Distorted images of what it used to be taunt me,
Statues stand tall and proud yet deserted and worn.

A dilapidated well sits enchantingly silent,
Its treasures in secrets hidden in the darkness,
Mysterious cobwebs weave, enticing you,
Their bewitching webs drawing you ever closer.

The master of the willow trees stand majestic and grand,
His eyes engulfing me
And his gnarled branches reaching out to grasp me,
His wisdom seeps from every leaf like running water.

Sunlight weeps through thick canopy of trees,
As they whisper deep secrets to one another,
Like giants towering over you,
Glaring at you as if you were invisible.

The neglected, forlorn garden sits alone and depressed,
It was a garden,
A lost garden,
Like a labyrinth of lost dreams.

Lara Jesani (12)
St Martin's School, Solihull

I Wish

I wish
That I could be,
Anything but me.

Sitting, staring,
At nothing much that you can see.

You think that I just,
Stare out into space,
You see a cloud doesn't do much.

I just watch the world going by,
Making myself bigger then smaller day by day,
Making everyone miserable, or not some say.

I wish that just for once,
I could be something else,
A dragon that breathes fire,
A flower who likes the clouds.

But oh no, I just have to imagine,
I just have to pretend,
Trying to like people like me,
When they play games.

I like to hear them say,
'That cloud's a dragon,
No, it's a flower,'
Or 'I think it looks just
Like your mother.'

I wish I could be,
Something else for just a day,
I would like to make people like me,
Not hate me because of the rain.

I wish that I wasn't a cloud,
But something altogether different,
Something people would respect me for,
Like a king or a queen.

And maybe if I wish hard enough,
One day I will be.

Natasha Browne (11)
St Martin's School, Solihull

The Lost Garden

We are lurking in the darkness,
From behind you we're devouring,
We're watching, always watching,
Your end is coming.

Ivy is creeping up to your house
And slithering up the walls,
Smothering the windows,
Now you cannot see.

The trees so wise and old,
Tripping you with their gnarled roots,
Staring at you with their disfigured faces,
Choking you tenaciously.

Flowers are wilting,
We're tangling them together, they'll never be free,
They're calling you with their aroma,
But we're obliterating it with our odour.

The wind is whispering to you,
It's murmuring our curse,
Beckoning to you, daring you,
To come into our domain.

In the darkness we lurk,
From behind you we devour,
We're watching you, always watching,
Your end is near.

Victoria Currie (12)
St Martin's School, Solihull

The Angel

A sparkling crystal clear light,
Silky white the same as the moon,
So beautiful, so extraordinary,
So . . . different.

The angel, the perfect angel,
Flying, floating, falling like a leaf to the ground,
She is natural, pure, glowing with beauty,
Her silver halo hovering above her head making her seem
Special and important.

The angel so amazing, she makes people stop and stare,
Her eyes a shining blue,
Her long golden hair flowing past her shoulders
And her wings, slender and graceful as they carry her.

Her gorgeous white dress like the sea rippling down to her knees,
Her arms partly covered by creamy sleeves resting at her side,
Her pink ballet pumps hanging loosely on her feet
And her magical wand shimmering silver dangling from her hand.

She slowly, carefully comes down and kisses
People on the forehead,
Blesses those who are sad, scared and empty,
Then returning to the sky, the sparkling crystal light
Is back,
The angel, the splendid angel!

Jenny Hawkins (12)
St Martin's School, Solihull

Onyota A:Ka (The People Of The Standing Stone)

Our nations once stood proud and tall,
Wearing feathers, beads and bones,
We are the people of the standing stone.

We still exist,
Our nations are still here,
We live like you, with TV, pop music and computer games.

We keep our ways of standing tall, the way our ancestors did,
They taught us how to carry on,
We show our culture through a pow-wow,
There is a dance competition to be won.

Pow-wows are to help keep traditions alive,
They help our nations to survive,
They bring together everyone,
So that people can see what we've done.

Pow-wows are ways of expressing who we are,
To dance, to be creative,
To help others in need.

Helping others, in good times and bad,
This is what our ancestors taught us.

One day you may see a standing stone on the horizon,
Who will you think of?

Madison Cowell (11)
St Martin's School, Solihull

The Lost Garden

Lost was the garden,
That held so many secrets,
That once possessed the beauty of a god,
Neglected and antiquated it now stood,
Blanketed in a sheet of death.

Like a labyrinth of lost dreams,
Portraying distorted images,
Of how it used to be,
Bewitching me in its powerful spell.

The ancient willow tree stood,
Sad, dejected, as it
Glumly looked upon
Its dying kingdom of nature.

Lost was my beautiful garden,
Which held so many treasures,
Aware of its abandonment it
Braced itself for the arrival,
Of the bitter end.

Martha Ngatchu (12)
St Martin's School, Solihull

Young Writers Information

We hope you have enjoyed reading this book - and that you will continue to enjoy it in the coming years.

If you like reading and writing poetry drop us a line, or give us a call, and we'll send you a free information pack.

Alternatively if you would like to order further copies of this book or any of our other titles, then please give us a call or log onto our website at www.youngwriters.co.uk

Young Writers Information
Remus House
Coltsfoot Drive
Peterborough
PE2 9JX

(01733) 890066